the ARTIST'S RULE

In a world that lives in the shallows, hungering for depth, meaning, and beauty, *The Artist's Rule* entices us to plunge into the riches of a contemplative, creative life. With hospitality, wisdom, and grace, Christine Valters Paintner returns us to ancient monastic practices that have preserved the soul of spirituality across the ages and can restore us in our own time. Silence, solitude, sacred reading, stillness: such treasures of the monastic path have the power to transform us and draw us far into the mysteries that lie at the heart of our lives. As she illuminates and navigates the connections between contemplation and the act of creation, Paintner beckons us into a sacred threshold space. What we find in this space—this sanctuary—will sustain and deepen our creative call, for the life of the world.

Jan L. Richardson
Author of *In the Sanctuary of Women*

I highly recommend *The Artist's Rule* as a way to explore and embrace our inner monk and inner artist so we can unleash greater creative living. Using the wisdom of Benedictine values, Christine Valters Paintner seeks to nurture contemplative and expressive practices that flow from seeing all of life as a sacred, creative gift we give each other. Inner contemplative practices yield and sustain a creative, expressive life and enable us to see our world as holy.

Lucy Wynkoop, O.S.B.
Coauthor of *Lectio Divina: Contemplative Awakening and Awareness*

Graciously offered, wisely conceived, carefully crafted, *The Artist's Rule* leads the reader ever more deeply into practices that recover the awareness that contemplation and creativity spring from the same Source. This work, grounded in Benedictine spirituality, offers us ways to rediscover the sacred art of living and serving, following the Spirit's lead and awakening to the artist's palette of our daily lives.

Mary C. Earle
Author of *The Desert Mothers*

In *The Artist's Rule*, Christine Valters Paintner offers a helpful recipe for living a contemplative life. In a series of chapters intended for use over a twelve-week period, she presents gentle yet challenging invitations to deepen one's commitment to creativity and prayerful presence to the world, through a careful and wise selection of thoughts for reflection paired with practical activities to engage body as well as spirit.

Norvene Vest
Author of *Friend of the Soul*

This book is for all artists and budding artists who long for an infusion of creative spirit. By melding monastic practices of embodied spirituality with fresh invitations for creating art, Paintner shows how to make creative life out of your whole life.

Margaret D. McGee
Author of *Haiku—The Sacred Art*

It is a time of shift, of awakening, new challenges, greater complexity in every dimension of daily life. *The Artist's Rule* is a treasure for those of us who long to live a rich inner life, to be fully human and creative members of a creative Universe, to give expression to what is moving within us—to write, paint, make music, and dance. Christine frames her exploration in monastic wisdom, but in our present context where the whole world is our monastery.

The inner guide of each of us is thoroughly welcomed and nourished throughout these chapters—in explorations, guided imagery, mystical insight, poetry, music, reflections, inspiration, practices of creativity, and ritual—as we travel today's call to creativity and contemplation.

Mary Southard, C.S.J.
Artist and illustrator for *The Cosmic Dance*

Benedict established a school for God's service, intending his monastery to be a place where seekers learn how to incarnate God's awesome presence in our midst and to embody the Good News to others. *The Artist's Rule* does just this, guiding us into very human practices that help us cultivate deeper awareness of our relationship to the Divine. These spiritual practices will support our growth into our humanity. And they're just fun! I highly recommend Christine's work.

Laura Swan, O.S.B.
Author of *Engaging Benedict*

Monastic practices are not just for monks; living a creative life is not just for professional artists. Christine Valters Paintner teaches us these truths as a wise, gentle guide who knows when to speak and when to get out of the way. With her help, we open ourselves to the Mystery at the heart of life, and in so doing come to know ourselves more deeply and to bring forth our gifts for others.

Jane Redmont
Author of *When in Doubt, Sing*

This is not your standard contemplative practice. Be ready to be rocked, to be pulled and pushed, and to fly. This book is like an angel who sweetly whispers to the ear of my heart "create (draw, sketch, paint, move, cook, hum, write, be silent) to praise." This book helps me to embody the Benedictine motto: "That in everything, we glorify God."

Roy DeLeon, Obl. O.S.B.
Author of *Praying with the Body*

the ARTIST'S RULE

A TWELVE-WEEK JOURNEY

CHRISTINE VALTERS PAINTNER

author of *Water, Wind, Earth, & Fire*

nurturing your creative soul
with monastic wisdom

SORIN BOOKS  Notre Dame, Indiana

"How to Be a Poet" by Wendell Berry, copyright © 1998, from *The Selected Poems of Wendell Berry,* is used by permission of Counterpoint Press.

"I Am Going to Start Living Like a Mystic" from *Lay Back the Darkness: Poems,* by Edward Hirsch, copyright © 2003 by Edward Hirsch. Used by permission of Alfred A. Knopf, a division of Random House, Inc.

"Instructions" by Sheri Hostetler from *A Cappella: Mennonite Voices in Poetry,* edited by Ann Hostetler, copyright © 2003, is used by permission of University of Iowa Press.

---

www.sorinbooks.com

ISBN-10 1-933495-29-4   ISBN-13 978-1-933495-29-3

Cover image © iStock.

Cover and text design by Brian C. Conley.

Printed and bound in the United States of America.

Library of Congress Cataloging-in-Publication Data
Paintner, Christine Valters.
  The artist's rule : nurturing your creative soul with monastic wisdom / Christine Valters Paintner.
    p. cm.
  ISBN-13: 978-1-933495-29-3 (pbk.)
  ISBN-10: 1-933495-29-4 (pbk.)
1. Creation (Literary, artistic, etc.)--Religious aspects--Christianity--Meditations.
2. Benedict, Saint, Abbot of Monte Cassino. Regula. 3. Creative ability--Problems, exercises, etc. I. Title.
  BV4596.A78P35 2011
  248.3'40887--dc22

                    2011015475

To the Benedictine Sisters and

Oblates of St. Placid Priory,

who support and sustain me in

living the monastic path

each and every day.

CONTENTS

FOREWORD

And don't we all, with fierce hunger, crave a cave of solitude,
a space of deep listening—full of quiet darkness and stars,
until finally we hear a syllable of God
echoing in the cave of our hearts?

—Macrina Wiederkehr

When Benedict of Nursia abandoned his studies in Rome, he found his way to a cave in the hills of Subiaco. This cave would become his *sacro speco* (sacred space), for it was there that Benedict devoted three years of his life to searching for God. Out of his deep listening in the cave of solitude was born one of the most loved rules of all ages—the Rule of St. Benedict.

The Artist's Rule has the potential of becoming your own *sacro speco*. Just as Benedict spent three years of solitude in a cave, you're invited by this inspiring work to spend twelve weeks in the cave of your heart, nurturing your creative soul, and sitting at the feet of your inner monk.

The monk, a universal archetype of the search for the divine, represents everything in you that leans toward the sacred, all that reaches for what is eternal. The monk represents everything within you that is drawn to seek with unwavering love; to wait for the Holy One with reverential awe; to praise, bow, and adore.

The artist speaks to that part of you which yearns for beauty and creativity. Your inner artist invites you to participate in the great work of healing the world by lifting out of your senses creative images, words, and actions that inspire others to live lives of wonder and surprise.

Christine Valters Paintner's joyous spirit and love for the monastic way shines through her teaching as she describes the various ways the tools of the monk can become tools for the artist. The Benedictine vows of stability, conversion, and obedience can become a staff of support, leading you to a greater faithfulness to your creative soul.

Both the monk and the artist have fundamental voices that are needed for the transformation of our world.

Although many writers have tried to help us open the door to our creativity, *The Artist's Rule* seems unique in revealing to us a special kinship between the monk and the artist. The threads of monastic wisdom woven through these pages can serve as an "endowment fund." Dip into this sacred reservoir when you need the discipline to align your heart's desires with your actions.

Having had the good fortune of being a participant in Christine's online course, *Way of the Monk, Path of the Artist*, I know from experience that the artist and monk cannot be hurried. An artist who hurries has lost his original integrity. A monk who hurries has lost a little of her soul. Both monk and artist are teachers of the contemplative way.

This jewel of a book will help you tap the eternal in your soul. Let the monk and the artist, who have always been your silent companions, lead you to your inner monastery and to your inner art studio. Christine will be your trustworthy guide.

Macrina Wiederkehr, O.S.B.
Monk of St. Scholastica Monastery
Fort Smith, Arkansas

ACKNOWLEDGMENTS

I carry a heart overflowing with gratitude to the following people who helped to make this book possible:

My husband John, who continues to support all of my creative and contemplative work with such enthusiasm and care. Thank you my beloved, I am deeply blessed by your love for me.

The Benedictine community of St. Placid Priory in Lacey, Washington, especially Sister Lucy Wynkoop, who is both Oblate Director and dear friend, and my fellow oblates, who help make living out the Benedictine way in the world a wonder-filled experience of daily discovery.

The participants in my online *Way of the Monk, Path of the Artist* course, who helped nurture the seeds of this work through their unbridled enthusiasm and wholehearted engagement with the process. I am especially grateful to the following people who granted permission for me to publish their poems in this book: Anne Buck, Laurie Kathleen Clark, Kayce S. Hughlett, Cathleen Johnson, Yvonne M. Lucia, Suzie Kline Massey, Cheryl MacPherson, Eveline Maedel, Tess Giles Marshall, Barbara Miller, Lynn Penney, Rebecca Piskura, Laurel Pritchard, Cindy Read, Melinda Schwakhofer, Judy Smoot, Deb Swingholm, Lynn Ungar, Macrina Wiederkehr, Stacy Wills, and Edward C. Zaragoza. The permission is for use in this book alone and the poems may not be further duplicated without their permission. I also want to thank the members of the Sacred Order of Monks

xiv   *the* ARTIST'S RULE

and Artists (SOMA), who continue to live out the integration of contemplative and creative ways of being in beautiful ways.

Betsey Beckman and Kayce Stevens Hughlett, who are my cherished teaching and playing partners and friends, and who encourage me in my own creative explorations.

Cindy Read; Suzie (Shira) Kline Massey; June Mears Driedger; Judy Smoot; Lucy Wynkoop, O.S.B.; Ted Zaragoza; and Stacy Stall Wills; who read a draft of this manuscript and offered invaluable input and feedback; and Tess Giles Marshall, who helped inspire some of the material in the chapter on work.

Robert Hamma and Susanna Cover, the fine editors at Ave Maria Press, who help to make the process of bringing a book to publication full of ease and joy.

CLAIMING MONASTIC GIFTS
for CREATIVE LIVING

The heart of human identity is the capacity and desire for birthing.
To be is to become creative and bring forth the beautiful.

—JOHN O'DONOHUE

You may be coming to this book as an artist or writer seeking spiritual practices to help ground and support your creative expression. Or you may be someone who is already familiar with the treasures of monastic tradition, but are looking for another window into this way of life. Perhaps you have intuitively known the connections between contemplative practice and creative expression, and this book will feel like coming home.

Amid so many titles about monastic spirituality and about creativity, this book sheds a new light on both by demonstrating monastic practices as valuable ways to encourage and sustain a creative life. What I have discovered in my own journey is that the contemplative path allows my creativity to flourish in ways it never did before I embraced monastic practice. This book is for anyone who longs for ways to more deeply integrate his or her spiritual path and creative longings.

Discovering the monastic way has been one of the great joys of my life. Years ago I thought the life of monks had nothing substantial to offer me in the world beyond the monastery walls. While growing up in New

York City, I came to love the city's museums. One of my favorites was The Cloisters, a branch of The Metropolitan Museum of Art on the north end of Manhattan overlooking the Hudson River. It was created from elements of five different medieval French monasteries. I loved wandering the cool stone hallways, gazing at the pages of illuminated manuscripts, admiring the unicorn tapestries, sitting in the peace and refreshment of the medieval garden. I was not aware of it consciously at the time, but the aesthetic dimension of monasticism had captured my heart long before I knew about the contemplative wisdom and rhythms of prayer that would one day become my spiritual home.

While I was in graduate school, I became enamored with Hildegard of Bingen, the twelfth-century Benedictine abbess who was an artist, visionary, musician, theologian, preacher, spiritual director, and healer. Her sheer creative breadth captivated me. I felt a kinship to her expansive spirit. She could be a wisdom guide for me across time. I grew curious about the context of her life and what supported her creative flourishing. As the abbess of a Benedictine community, she was, of course, deeply immersed in monastic life and practices, and so my interest in her life became the doorway into my passion for Benedictine spirituality. The Rule of St. Benedict, written 1500 years ago, offers balanced and profound wisdom for living a contemplative, spirit-centered life even in today's complex world.

Through Hildegard's guidance, I discovered that the way of the monk is connected to my path as an artist and writer. Monks have been the great preservers of literary tradition, saving many sacred texts from destruction and loss during the Middle Ages and illuminating manuscripts with gorgeous art. They have offered their gifts in the service of creating beautiful spaces of sanctuary. Monasticism has given us the great tradition of chant to immerse us in the continuous cascade of praying the Liturgy of the Hours. These ways of being in the world have been cultivated over hundreds of years of practice and offer us tremendous wisdom about what it means to live a meaningful, vital, and creative life.

When my husband and I moved to Seattle after graduate school and I knew it would be home for a while, I made the journey toward becoming a Benedictine oblate. An oblate is a layperson or clerical member who makes a commitment to the prayer life and spirituality of a particular monastery, and to live out its way of life in her or his circumstances.

St. Placid Priory is a community of sisters, situated about an hour from where I live. The sisters and my fellow oblates offer me tremendous support in living contemplatively in the world. I have a deep love of Benedictine tradition, as well as the gifts of Celtic and desert monasticism. The monastic way is my primary path through the world and the foundation of my work in spiritual formation, direction, and teaching.

Twelve-Week Journey

A New Moon teaches gradualness and deliberation and how one gives birth to oneself slowly. Patience with small details makes perfect a large work, like the universe. What nine months of attention does for an embryo forty early mornings will do for your gradually growing wholeness.

—Rumi

This book began as an online course called *Way of the Monk, Path of the Artist*. The material had been ripening in me for months; and when I finally offered it as a course, I was deeply moved by the enthusiastic response. Teaching this material has been a marvelous way to refine the writing of this book. I have had the privilege of witnessing participants as they integrate monastic wisdom into their lives, engage in the creative explorations in each chapter, and deepen into a creative and contemplative way of being in the world. At the end of each chapter of this book, you will find poems written by some of the participants in response to the material.

I chose twelve weeks for this process because it is the span of a season. Seasonal cycles are very important to this work and offer wisdom for cultivating creative rhythms, which we will explore later in the book. Monastic tradition has taught me the treasure offered in the rise and fall of each day and the invitation to tend the gift and quality of each moment.

As you begin this journey, I invite you to make a commitment to your inner monk and artist, to cultivate space for each to flourish, and to see what they have to offer to your creative and contemplative paths. Each chapter in this book is designed to be explored over a week's time and focuses on a different aspect of monastic spirituality. The content illuminates the ways contemplative practice can support creative work through the practice of *lectio divina*, reflection questions, meditations, and art explorations that include suggestions for visual art, poetry, music, and movement.

My background and training is in the expressive arts—which originally developed within the psychotherapeutic field. This approach engages the arts for healing and discovery while focusing on the process more than the product. When we move from one art medium to another, we encounter deeper wisdom through access to multiple languages and ways of knowing. John Daido Loori, the author of *The Zen of Creativity: Cultivating Your Artistic Life*, writes: "The creative process, like a spiritual journey, is intuitive, non-linear, and experiential. It points us toward our essential nature, which is a reflection of the boundless creativity of the universe." Creativity and contemplative spirituality nurture and support each other in their commitments to the slow way, to a close attention to the inner life, and to the sacred being revealed in each moment. When I use the word "artist" I include poets, writers, cooks, gardeners, and people who use all manner of creative expression; we are all called to be artists of everyday life.

There is nothing magical about the particular set of practices, meditations, and art explorations I suggest; they are offered as invitations and possibilities, doorways to explore the creative qualities of particular monastic values and virtues. You are invited to engage the ones with which you feel resonance, and if some evoke dissonance, I invite you to consider engaging those as well, while paying attention to what your response reveals about your inner life. An important part of the monastic way is to engage the places of our lives that challenge us and even make us bristle. The transformation comes from engaging in the work, of practicing being present to the moment and what it has to teach you about yourself, your creative process, and God. Showing up each day with gentleness and compassion is the heart of the path.

In week one, through silence and solitude, you are invited to establish a creative, contemplative practice of the ancient art of *lectio divina*—or "sacred reading." You are invited as well to walk as a practice of being present to the world. The focus of week two is considering the archetypes of the inner monk and inner artist, which we all have within us. The work of week three draws on the monastic practice of seeing all things as holy—regarding the tools of the monastery as sacred implements. When you bring this awareness to your work as an artist or writer, your pen and brush become vessels of awareness of God at work. During week four, I explore the sacred rhythms of the Liturgy of the Hours as an invitation into creative rhythms for inspiration and renewal. During week five, I examine three of the commitments that Benedictine monks make—to the virtues of stability, conversion, and obedience—as the backbone of a commitment to the creative life. The focus of week six is to embrace the monastic virtue of humility as a way to explore creative gifts, blocks, and limitations and allow yourself to release perfection.

During week seven, consider the monastic practice of hospitality as welcoming the stranger both outside and inside yourself. An intentional practice of hospitality calls you to make room within yourself for all the inner voices that rise up in your creative process and contemplative prayer. The work of week eight invites deeper contemplation of your need for a community of support. During week nine, we embrace the invitation of Celtic monasticism to regard nature as a source of divine revelation and inspiration for our work as artists. The focus of week ten is to reflect on the desert way of simplicity and to examine how letting go can make more room for creative expression. In week eleven, you explore creative work as a vocation to holy service in the world and consider the value of creativity in the world. We complete this work with week twelve and the creation of an artist's "rule of life" as an articulation of your ongoing commitments to practice. Rather than a stringent set of stifling rules, a rule of life is a set of wisdom guidelines for how to live in a meaningful way. Of course, the spiritual journey is always a work in progress, and so the invitation beyond these twelve weeks is to bring this new awareness to the rest of your life.

How to Work with This Book

I recommend working your way through the book sequentially, week by week. You might consider journeying together with a friend or a spiritual director, forming a group where you live, or engaging in online support at my website, www.AbbeyoftheArts.com. There is great power in engaging in these experiences and much beauty in having those experiences witnessed in a loving way by another person. Each chapter includes reflections on the topic, a passage for praying with lectio divina, and two art explorations—generally a visual and written experience, but sometimes gentle movement instead. Many of the chapters include scripts for guided meditations. If it is helpful for you to have a guide in the process, consider recording the meditation for your prayer later in the week. You might also consider extending your engagement with these chapters over twelve months instead, working through each theme slowly over a year. Choose the rhythm that will sustain you in integrating the material.

As you begin, consider designating some time each week to read the reflection, practice lectio divina, engage in a walking meditation, and experience the art, poetry, and movement explorations. For these twelve weeks I suggest you block out some time each day—perhaps a half hour—to be present to your inner monk and artist, and a longer block each week—up to two hours—to reflect and enter into the experiences. When resistance arises, be gentle with yourself and notice what it has to say to you.

Most of all, this book is meant to be experienced. Reading through will give you intellectual understanding of the material. Engaging in the exercises, reflections, and practices at the end of each chapter will help you integrate the material into your life holistically.

Beginner's Mind and Heart

In his *Rule*, St. Benedict wisely writes that "always we begin again." I have found these four simple words to be of endless comfort in my own journey, a gentle reminder that I am called to recommit myself to the spiritual path again and again. I have never strayed so far away that I can't return to the loving embrace of the source of all creation. The thirteenth-century Sufi poet Rumi expresses a similar invitation:

> *Come, come, whoever you are.*
> *Wanderer, worshipper, lover of leaving.*
> *It doesn't matter.*
> *Ours is not a caravan of despair.*
> *Come, even if you have broken your vow*
> *a hundred times.*
> *Come, yet again, come, come.*

Buddhist monastic tradition also invites us into the practice of "beginner's mind." Bringing the mind and heart of a beginner to our lives helps us to discover the wisdom offered in each moment. When we let go of our desire to be clever or successful or to create beautiful things, we may begin to be open to the sacred truth of our experience as it is, not how we want it to be.

The purpose of this book is to invite you into a process of transformation. As you take up the practices I describe, try not to set a particular goal for yourself other than showing up to what is offered and being open to the experience. Expectation can preclude the opportunity for discovery. When we try to reach a goal, we become fixated on it and we miss the process. "Beginner's mind" is the practice of coming to an experience with an openness and a willingness to be transformed. Art can reconnect us with our childlike sense of wonder. When we engage art as prayer, we can remember that play is also an act of prayer, praising God out of sheer delight. We can learn to take ourselves—our art and our spirituality—a little less seriously.

The time ahead is filled with the riches of monastic practices and the delights of creative expression. I am honored to be your guide on this sacred journey.

ESTABLISHING *a* CREATIVE, CONTEMPLATIVE PRACTICE

*There is in us an instinct for newness, for renew-
al, for a liberation of creative power. We seek
to awaken in ourselves a force which really
changes our lives from within. And yet the same
instinct tells us that this change is a recovery of
that which is deepest, most original, most personal in ourselves. To be born again is not to
become somebody else, but to become ourselves.*

—THOMAS MERTON

As we begin, I want to take a moment to encourage you to check in with yourself regularly during these next few weeks of journeying through this material. One of the most important things I can teach is learning to make space to listen to your own deepest longings and to begin to trust those more. There are all kinds of reasons we learn to doubt ourselves, especially when it comes to artistic expression. Part of growth is taking risks, so I encourage boldness, but I equally encourage gentleness with yourself. When you begin a creative adventure like this—which is an extension of the journey you've already begun—you open yourself to your vulnerability, to the dreams just beginning to bud within, to the risk inherent in expressing your deepest self. There may be weeks where things feel more tender and you need to hold back just a little. Give yourself permission to do this.

My training in the arts is in the field of expressive arts, which engages creativity for self-expression, healing, and transformation. Through this lens, the process of art-making becomes a place of sacred discovery. When I make suggestions for the weekly creative exercises—in visual art, poetry, and movement—I encourage you to enter into the experience as a prayer, a communion with your Creative Source, and to see if you can release your worries about making a beautiful product. As an authentic expression of your longings and unique soul, what you make inevitably will have its own beauty.

There is certainly a place for the role of craft and fine art, and many of you may already be involved with the fine-art or craft world. Our focus here, however, is on the process rather than the product and on allowing the expression to come through as fully and authentically as possible. When judgments arise in the process, simply notice them with curiosity and compassion and contemplate where else in your life those voices arise. (I will address this far more extensively in the chapter on inner hospitality.) Allow the art-making process to become a container for your internal awareness, much like in meditation practice. The same is true for writing: allow yourself to express whatever is true for you in the process and, gently and with compassion for yourself, notice where the blocks, judgments, and voices arise. Give yourself permission to make mistakes, to make "bad art," or to write something that doesn't sound even close to perfect. This is the way we begin to cultivate inner freedom, by allowing ourselves a full range of expression as a journey of discovery.

Each time you begin an art experience, make some time to quiet yourself and connect to your breath, heartbeat, and body. Move into a receptive posture of stillness, which helps to quiet the judging mind and opens you to the gifts being offered. Each time you complete an art exploration or a prayer experience, offer thanks for this time spent with your inner monk or artist, and allow your heart to fill with gratitude for whatever wisdom has been revealed. The way of the monk and the path of the artist are teachers of slowness, of savoring, of seeing the world below surfaces.

Notice what the art materials themselves have to teach you in a given experience. Be present to the tactile qualities of collage and paint, of writing and movement, and what each one stirs or challenges in you. Allow this awareness to be a part of paying attention to the inner process.

Honoring Beginnings

A new beginning! We must learn to live each day, each hour, yes, each minute as a new beginning, as a unique opportunity to make everything new. Imagine that we could live each moment as a moment pregnant with new life. Imagine that we could live each day as a day full of promises. Imagine that we could walk through the new year always listening to a voice saying to us: "I have a gift for you and can't wait for you to see it! Imagine!"

—HENRI J.M. NOUWEN

This journey on which you are embarking represents a new beginning—a new or deepened commitment in your own life. Take just a moment to imagine you are crossing a threshold into an unexplored room of your soul. The great Spanish Carmelite mystic St. Teresa of Avila described such a spiritual journey as a movement through concentric rooms of an interior castle until we reach the diamond at the center of our being. She says when we reach this diamond we will finally realize how truly beautiful we really are. Feel the anticipation and savor the delight at being alive and full of the hope that leads you to explore the rich tradition of monastic practice. Simply pause and breathe. Breathe in and feel the possibility in this moment. Exhale and release the distractions. Breathe in and experience the expansion in your body as a reflection of the expansion in your spirit. Exhale and surrender yourself to this moment. Now pause and reflect on what it was about this book that made your heart say yes. What were the words, the images, the ideas that touched something in you? Notice if there is a word or image right now that symbolizes what is rising up in you, and linger with it for as long as feels satisfying. Consider recording it in a journal using color and shape.

The Inner Monastery

The true monastery was not dependent on the enclosure of walls. It was, rather, a quality of consciousness or a state of heart that involved daily commitment to maintain an inner aloneness—that place where God and soul dwell in intimacy.

—BEVERLY LANZETTA

In her book *Radical Wisdom,* Beverly Lanzetta describes medieval monasticism, and her words about the true monastery being a quality of consciousness apply equally today. Perhaps with more and more people beyond the walls of enclosure seeking the gifts of the contemplative life, cultivating this state of heart is more important than ever. She later writes that in contemporary life, such consciousness means remembering that the inner monastery is the ground from which all of our life extends—and I would emphasize that this includes creative expression:

> Contemplation is always a revolutionary act. It subverts the daily tedium and searches for the kernel of meaning hidden at the center of each thing. . . . The stone enclosure that literally marked the boundaries of the medieval monastery is transposed from the concrete into a state or quality of consciousness. To be enclosed in the monastic sense is to devote oneself to God. In a modern context, this ancient purity of heart refers to the discovery of the divine as the one relationship fundamentally essential to one's life and lives out of its sources. . . . To find the monastery within is to discover the place of rest out of which all other relations flourish and grow.

The inner monastery is a quality of consciousness you bring to everything you do, including creating. It is the crucible for your transformation, and everything you need to be whole is right there within you already.

The desert monks would say, "Sit in your cell, and it will teach you everything" (Thomas Merton, *Wisdom of the Desert*). This cell is the cave of your heart, that interior place of reflection and struggle. It is the place where the spark of the divine glows and you carry that with you wherever you go. As you make art or write, the process is a container for awareness. Everything that rises up—judgments, blocks, and insights—is a reflection of the whole of your life. Your cell, the blank canvas, the white page— each of these invites you to pay attention to what is happening right in this moment. There is no need to go elsewhere to find enlightenment or transformation. The space within which you dwell and the container for your creative expression can each become the holy site of struggle and freedom. Whatever you encounter in prayer and art making is a micro- cosm of the macrocosm of your life:

> You do not need to leave your room. . . . Remain sitting
> at your table and listen. Do not even listen, simply wait.
> Do not even wait, be quite still and solitary. The world will
> freely offer itself to you to be unmasked. It has no choice. It
> will roll in ecstasy at your feet. (Franz Kafka)

Silence and Solitude

Silence is never merely the cessation of words. . . .
Rather it is the pause that holds together—indeed,
it makes sense of—all the words, both spoken and
unspoken. Silence is the glue that connects our
attitudes and our actions. Silence is the fullness,
not emptiness; it is not absence, but the aware-
ness of a presence.

—JOHN CHRYSSAVGIS

An essential element of committing to the monastic way is cultivat- ing a place for silence and solitude. Like the rest at the end of a busy week that comes with Sabbath or the few moments of pause in the physical pose of *shavasana* at the end of a yoga practice, the nourishing dimension of silence is honored and uplifted across traditions. As Chryssavgis describes, silence is the element that holds everything together. Entering into silence means to enter into an encounter with the One who ushered us from the great silence, who spoke us into being out of the wide expanse of silent presence.

Silence can be challenging. Not just because the world we live in conspires to fill each moment with noise—from radios to televisions to movies to music to urban sounds of traffic and to the congestion of people living close together—but because there is also a fear of entering into silence. When we are used to living at a distance from our deep center—caught up in the surface chatter—dropping down into the silent pool of God's presence can evoke fearfulness. What might we discover when we pause long enough to really hear? And yet, as Thomas Merton wrote, we each have a "vocation to solitude." This vocation means:

> . . . to deliver oneself up, to hand oneself over, entrust oneself completely to the silence of a wide landscape of woods and hills, or sea, or desert; to sit still while the sun comes up over that land and fills its silences with light. To pray and work in the morning and to labour and rest in the afternoon, and to sit still again in meditation in the evening when night falls upon that land and when the silence fills itself with darkness and with stars. This is a true and special vocation. There are a few who are willing to belong completely to such silence, to let it soak into their bones, to breathe nothing but silence, to feed on silence, and to turn to the very substance of their life into a living and vigilant silence. (*Thoughts in Solitude*)

Silence isn't something we do, although we can still ourselves to receive its gifts. It is not a personal capacity, although we can cultivate practices of becoming more present. Meister Eckhart described silence as "the purest element of the soul, the soul's most exalted place, the core, the essence of the soul." This is the inner monastery within each of our hearts, a place of absolute stillness, our soul's deep essence.

I echo Merton's invitations here: let yourself belong to silence, let silence soak into your bones, nourish you, be the air you breathe. A commitment to silence is at the heart of nurturing a contemplative practice and creative life. In silence you will discover the Great Artist from whom you emerged; you will sense the pulse of creative energy through your being so that you slowly grow to recognize that creating is your birthright, and that you join your work with this ultimate work. But the call is nourished by the silence. We continue to return to this open space to remember who we are.

Establishing (or Deepening) a Contemplative, Creative Practice

I believe that we learn by practice. Whether it means to learn to dance by practicing dancing or to learn to live by practicing living, the principles are the same. In each, it is the performance of a dedicated precise set of acts, physical or intellectual, from which comes shape of achievement, a sense of one's being, a satisfaction of spirit. One becomes, in some area, an athlete of God. Practice means to perform, over and over again in the face of all obstacles, some act of vision, of faith, of desire. Practice is a means of inviting the perfection desired.

—MARTHA GRAHAM

What does it mean to practice the spiritual life? When we embody practices, we live into them and they shape our habits of being. We have to practice being present to the moment, because our tendency—and the world around us conspires in this—is to be distracted. The monk practices contemplation so that in her whole life she can become conscious of the sacred presence beating through the heart of the world. (While female monastics are often called nuns, in this book I use the term "monk" to include both men and women because I believe that the term is archetypal;

that is, the energy of monk exists within each one of us regardless of gender.) The artist practices creativity so that he can experience all of life as a work of art. In his *Letter to Artists*, John Paul II wrote: "Not all are called to be artists in the specific sense of the term. Yet, as Genesis has it, all men and women are entrusted with the task of crafting their own life: In a certain sense, they are to make of it a work of art, a masterpiece."

The primary creative act is the living of our daily lives, making of it a work of art. This happens through daily attention to practice. To be a writer you must write; to be an artist you must show up to the canvas. You may already have some practices that work effectively to support you in your creative expression and contemplative presence. St. Benedict prescribes *ora et labora*—prayer and work in balance. Praying the Liturgy of the Hours and lectio divina, doing manual labor, and sleeping comprise the majority of a monk's schedule. In this book we explore a variety of monastic practices to support creative living in balance.

To begin, I suggest the following three practices as ones that I have found to be essential for my own thriving as a monk and artist: walking, lectio divina, and reflection. I include these practices in some form each week and I invite you to consider making time for them.

Walking

Perhaps the truth depends on a walk around the lake.

—WALLACE STEVENS

Do not go where the path may lead, go instead where there is no path and leave a trail.

—RALPH WALDO EMERSON

St. Benedict prescribed manual labor as a part of his *Rule*. In large part, manual labor is included so that the monks can earn their living, but I think there is a deeper wisdom here about the need to engage the body on the spiritual journey. Many of us earn our livings through very sedentary and intellectual work and neglect our bodies' needs for movement. One of my primary spiritual practices is a contemplative walk each morning. This doesn't mean I necessarily walk slowly, although there is a whole Buddhist tradition of mindful slow walking that is quite powerful. For me, this walk is a way of honoring the seasons of the earth and of my soul. With each walk I listen for the invitation of the world around me. Walking is a way of arriving fully to the place I am in; it helps me to become present to this moment in time and discover the gifts hidden both within and without. The rhythm of walking connects me again to the primal rhythm of breath and heartbeat in my own body and pulsing throughout creation. When I find myself feeling stuck for ideas and inspiration or feeling like my perspective has narrowed from fatigue, a walk can change everything—creating shifts, renewal, and invigoration.

The contemplative dimension of walking comes through my presence to the world around me and to what is moving through me as I walk. I listen for the ways the divine is speaking through the world. I listen to my own heart beating more loudly because of the vigor of my movement. I listen for the ways that new ideas arise in this space.

The first practice I recommend is simply this: take a walk regularly, perhaps once a week or once each day if you can make the time. Listen for what feels life giving rather than imposing a "should" on yourself. Your walk might be a practice for the morning or evening as a way of being present to a particular hour of the day. (We will explore creative rhythms more fully in chapter 4.) Or it might be that you take a walk when you begin to notice yourself feeling stuck or blocked or when the inner voices seem to be speaking quite loudly. Take them for a walk and show them the wonders of the world and notice if they shift.

Begin your walk by taking a few moments to simply become present to your body and to gently move your awareness down into your heart center. I often place my hand on my heart to experience a physical connection and return to this gesture whenever I find myself thinking things through rather than allowing them to work on me. See if you can walk without needing to get anywhere in particular. As you take each step listen for the next invitation. Is there a tree or a crow calling for some attention? Allow time to simply be present to the way the world is inviting you into deeper attention to the gifts of this moment in time.

Lectio Divina

Lectio divina, or "sacred reading," is an ancient practice and can include any sacred text—a passage that moves you, a poem you love, or an image that is calling for your attention. I often combine my walking and lectio divina: I take a word with me on the walk and allow it to unfold, or I am present to nature and listen for the "word" which comes from creation. St. Benedict in his *Rule* required every monk to spend significant time each day in lectio divina as a contemplative way of being with scripture. The Carmelite William McNamara describes contemplation as a "long, loving look at the real." Contemplation is long, which means it takes time and requires us to slow ourselves down and create more spaciousness; contemplation is loving, which means that it is a heart-centered practice that calls us to expand our capacity for compassion; and contemplation is a look at the real, which means that we are called to gaze upon all of the world, both the beauty and the sorrow.

Benedict began his *Rule* with the phrase "Listen with the ear of your heart." The ear of the heart does not refer to our physical ear, but to the metaphorical center of our being where we make meaning. When we pray lectio, we are invited to move our awareness from a purely rational and analytical response to the text, and bring the whole of ourselves, including the intuitive and emotional side, to the process.

Lectio divina assumes that there is a depth dimension to scripture and that the story meets us right where we are in this moment, whatever our experience might be. Each time we pray in this way, we are a different person and so we meet the scriptures from this perspective. Scripture is filled with rich metaphors and images that can stir our imaginations. Lectio is a series of inner movements, which are more spiral than linear. We begin our practice by moving from step to step, allowing the progression to become a part of ourselves so that gradually the rhythm takes root and we can let it unfold in its own way.

These are the four primary movements of lectio divina. (The section "Contemplative Practices" at the end of this chapter provides more details.)

1. Read (*lectio*): read and listen for a word or phrase which calls to us in this moment.
2. Reflect (*meditatio*): savor the word and allow it to unfold within you.

3. Respond (*oratio*): listen for the invitation.
4. Rest (*contemplatio*): rest in stillness.

Like other meditation practices, lectio divina can become a container for awareness of inner movements and voices—what stirs in us during this time is a microcosm of our daily lives. As you pray lectio, notice any distractions and gently release them. Let go of self-judgment and return gently to your prayer. The regular practice of lectio can be a rich support for artists and writers because it encourages the release of the thinking mind and a presence to the wisdom of the heart as you open to feeling and imagination. Lectio is a time for listening to the invitations the Great Artist is offering to our lives.

Each week I offer a suggested text with which to pray lectio. Creativity is fundamentally about newness. When we create, we make something that wasn't there before, a new image or song, a new vision or arrangement of materials. God is the primary Creator, breathing life and newness into each of us, sustaining creation each day, offering new possibility at every turn. The English mystic Evelyn Underhill described God as the "Supreme Artist" and our creative action as the "living, ardent tool" with which the artist works. Both the Hebrew and Christian scriptures give us this promise of a new creation in each moment. We read, "I will give you a new heart and place a new spirit within you" (Ez 36:26), "when you are in Christ, you are a New Creation; the old has gone, the new is here and now!" (2 Cor 5:17), and God says "Behold, I make all things new!" (Rv 21:5).

Reflection and Journaling

During this twelve-week journey many things will be stirred in you—new ideas, inspirations, challenges, insights. I recommend a journal as a place to capture your observations and questions. In addition to your practice of walking and lectio, I suggest you commit to a longer time each week to read through the lesson and begin to ponder how the material is working in you. Reflect on the previous week and take note of the wisdom that has emerged from your experience. Each chapter also includes specific questions for reflection to deepen your pondering.

Contemplative Practices

Invitation

As you begin this journey, make some space in your schedule for the process. Commit to your inner monk and artist, and begin this week by moving into the practice of lectio divina, walking, and reflection. Gather together some art supplies and create a space to unleash your inner artist in the coming weeks.

Lectio Divina

You will be invited each week to pray with a text through lectio divina. Feel free to refer back to the guidelines (that follow) to support your process. During this first week I invite you to pray with this passage from Isaiah and see what you discover:

> *Now I am revealing new things to you*
> *Things hidden and unknown to you*
> *Created just now, this very moment.*
> *Of these things you have heard nothing until now.*
> *So that you cannot say, Oh yes, I knew this.*
>
> —ISAIAH 48:6–7

Preparation

Take some time to become fully present to the moment. Become conscious of your breathing and allow your breath to draw your awareness from your head down to your heart.

Lectio (listening for God's address)

In your initial encounter with the text, listen for a word or phrase that shimmers, beckons, addresses you, unnerves you, disturbs you, stirs you, seems especially ripe with meaning. Repeat this word or phrase to yourself in the silence.

Meditatio (receiving God's address)

Gently repeat the word or phrase to yourself, allowing it to interact with the feelings, images, memories, and symbols that come to you during this time. Allow the word or phrase that has spoken to you to unfold in your imagination and speak more deeply.

Oratio (responding to God's address)

Allow your whole being to become a prayer by the honest expression of your deepest thoughts, feelings, and desires in dialogue with God.

Attend to the way this word, phrase, feeling, or image connects with the context and situation of your life right now. How does it relate to what you have heard and seen this day? How does it connect with what is happening at home, at work, in your leisure time?

Take an extended time of exploring this connection (in thought, in a journal, in art [see week one: Visual Art Exploration], in movement). How is God present to you there? Is God calling you to anything in your present circumstances? Is there a challenge presented here?

Contemplatio (beholding God's beauty)

Take time for simply resting in God and offering gratitude for God's presence in this time of prayer.

Gently bring your awareness back to the room and make space for some brief reflection on your experience.

Reflection Questions

- What do you need to say "no" to in your life to make space for this commitment and time of prayer and creativity?
- What are the longings you bring to your time in this process? What hopes do you carry?
- How might you bring some deeper intention to this moment of beginning?

Visual Art Exploration

Creative Response to Lectio Divina

This first week I invite you to engage in a simple and playful exploration of art materials. Have some paper and crayons, markers, or colored pencils available. Return to the passage from Isaiah (on page 20) and read it again. As you pray with this scripture passage, consider writing on the paper the word that stirs in you, choosing a color that calls to you and perhaps adding some playful design elements around it.

Then read it a second time following again the instructions for *meditatio*. As the memories, images, and feelings unfold, use color and shape to express some of what is moving in your prayer. In different colors add various symbols and borders around your initial word. Just let the expression unfold without judgment; let it be a prayer and journey of discovery.

Then read it a third time, following the instructions for the step of *oratio*. Pause for a longer period of exploration in color. Notice what God's invitation to you in this scripture text feels like, looks like; explore even the senses of smell and taste and sound. This moment of the third reading is about responding to the invitation God has placed in your heart. How might you respond in shape and color? How might the images emerging on the page be an extension of your listening for God's voice and paying attention to the call emerging from the initial word?

Sharing Secrets
The Monk tends the edges
And graces the borders of the in-between
He sees the hidden worlds between worlds
Walks in the shadowy lands
Amid awake and asleep
The Artist lifts the veils
And reveals beauty that would go unseen
She sees inside the creases and crevices
Unfolds the color of flowers
Puts scent on canvas
Together they play
Dancing on the narrow edge
Of time

That is NOW
They greet the present moment
Brushing past each other
Sharing secrets

—DEB SWINGHOLM

EXPLORING YOUR
INNER MONK *and* INNER ARTIST

True contemplation always overflows into cre-
ation—it becomes a creative act.

— BEVERLY LANZETTA

On Being a Monk and Artist

This is the invitation extended to—let us be so
bold as to say this—the new monk. The new
monk, who will never enter traditional institu-
tions, is yet impelled by the attractions of a life
built upon principles that are thoroughly monas-
tic. Our path requires, as an initiation into a new
(or renewed) way of life, a different conscious-
ness. We must disrupt old ways, shattering the
planes upon which we have unwittingly built
lives that do not bring us the happiness, the ful-
fillment, the transcendence for which we hunger.
We need not turn our back and flee to the monas-
tery; rather we must turn toward the world, our

*lives, our work, our community, our loved ones,
in a new way.*

—PAUL WILKES

The monastic way and artist's path are both ways of being in the world and journeying through life. The monk and artist each represent an archetype. Archetypes are psychological structures that are reflected in the symbols, images, and themes common across cultures and time periods. Archetypes reflect different energies working within us. We each contain a multiplicity of selves. This becomes most obvious to us when we experience an inner conflict of desires. Perhaps our desire for a more creative life feels like it is in conflict with our desire for financial security. Or our desire for a more contemplative life conflicts with the part of ourselves that loves to get everything done. One of these desires is not necessarily better than the other; at its root each desire teaches us something about ourselves and our deeper longings. Later in the course we will apply the monastic principle of hospitality to making room within ourselves for the full spectrum of inner dialogue. But for now, we focus on the two aspects that drew you to this book: the inner monk and the inner artist.

The inner monk seeks God as the source of all being, searches for a mystical connection to the Divine Source, longs for what is most essential in life, and cultivates this through a commitment to spiritual practice. The monk is nourished through silence and a commitment to see everything as sacred.

The inner artist engages the world through the senses and is passionate about beauty, seeking to express it through a variety of media (including visual art, poetry, movement, song, gardening, cooking, relationships, etc.). Artists bring a sense of wonder to their work and open up new ways of seeing the world.

In this book, we are essentially exploring what it means to be a "new monk"—one who lives beyond the monastery walls but brings the gifts and graces of monastic tradition to everyday life. We are also discovering what it is to be a "new artist"—one who seeks to satisfy a deep longing of the soul by making space for the delight and passion of creativity. These two paths meet in several places. Both monk and artist:

- cultivate a contemplative capacity for seeing the world beyond the surface appearances;
- welcome in awe, wonder, and holy curiosity as nourishment for the journey and as the seeds for new visions;
- live on the edges and in border spaces;
- serve the mysteries of the world.

We have explored contemplative practice already in the first chapter. Let's briefly explore these other aspects.

Awe, Wonder, and Holy Curiosity

Curiosity has its own reason for existing. One cannot help but be in awe when he contemplates the mysteries of eternity, of life, of the marvelous structure of reality. It is enough if one tries merely to comprehend a little of this mystery every day. Never lose a holy curiosity.

— ALBERT EINSTEIN

Have you ever seen the film *Children of Men* starring Clive Owen and Michael Caine? It is a bleak window into a future chaotic world in which no children have been born for eighteen years. A young black woman becomes pregnant and there is a race to protect and save her. For me, the whole movie was worth one scene near the end where the new mother walks down the stairs of a ramshackle building. She is carrying her newborn infant. War is raging around them. People try to take cover inside the building while police and military men storm in. She tries to keep her tiny child hidden and quiet, but the baby is crying and ultimately, is found beneath her cloak.

There is a beautiful and perfectly poignant moment as she walks down the stairs, past the men with their guns. You must remember that no one has seen an infant for eighteen long years. There has not been any sound of babies crying, no young fresh skin revealed to the world, no promise of newness as the world descends into chaos. As the woman walks past them, the uniformed soldiers all pause in a moment of rapturous wonder and awe. One man crosses himself at this holy sight. Then, just as quickly, the scene returns to violence behind her.

This moment has stayed with me in the months since I watched it. It speaks to the desperate need for moments of awe in the midst of a world caught up in chaos. It makes me wonder about the places in my own life where I have neglected the celebration of new life. It heartens me because I felt like that moment mattered, despite the return to violence in the film. Awe is a sign of allowing ourselves to be touched by beauty's transcendent quality. Wonder connects us to a childlike openness, to the world's possibilities. Holy curiosity calls us to remember that mystery is at the heart of the world. It calls us to break out of our tired vision of life.

I believe that beauty, as the great writer Fyodor Dostoyevsky observed, will indeed save the world. Beauty opens our heart wide like the lotus blossom, and we are slowly transformed. In this way, we are responsible for cultivating beauty in the world wherever we are, to participate in the world's transformation. This is our call as monks and artists.

Living in Border Spaces

Come to the edge, He said. They said: we are afraid.
Come to the edge, He said.
They came. He pushed them, and they flew . . .

—Guillaume Apollinaire

Both the monk and artist are edge dwellers, ones who commit to living in fertile border spaces and who call the wider community to alternative ways of being beyond the status quo. This can be a challenging and sometimes lonely place; it can also be exhilarating and exciting to step into the unknown. Living on the edges means recognizing those places and experiences that do not offer easy answers, those fierce edges of life where things are not as clear as we hope them to be. There is also beauty in the border spaces, those places of ambiguity and mystery. In *To Pause at the Threshold,* Esther de Waal writes that the ability to live with uncertainty requires courage and the need to ask questions more than to find answers.

Both monk and artist are called to hold the space for mystery within, and to dare to imagine new possibilities that are not yet fully formed. They are called to discover the new questions needing to be asked. They are called to listen to the new thing being formed right in this moment. The passage from Isaiah in our week one lectio practice reminds us of this calling.

In *Living on the Border of the Holy,* L. William Countryman writes that this border country is one we all carry within us. There is a fault line running down the middle of our lives that connects our ordinary reality with its deeper roots. The border country, he argues, is what gives our lives meaning:

> This border country is a place of intense vitality. It does not so much draw us away from the everyday world as it plunges us deeper into a reality of which the everyday world is like the surface. . . . To live there for a while is like having the veils pulled away.

Threshold space opens us up to life that is dynamic, intense, and often uncertain. Borders and edges are the places of transformation that call us to something deeper. Pulling away the veils means seeing the heart of things—which always demands a response. As monks and artists, we are called to slow down and see the world more deeply, to plunge ourselves fully into its heart, and to reveal what we discover.

Serving the Mysteries

> *I define religion at its best as a positive and effective means of relating to the mysteries that define our lives: love, death, birth, illness, marriage, and work, to name a few. . . . A twenty-first century religion sanctifies them with sacraments, rituals, sacred stories, and sometimes guardian*

spirits. The arts serve this kind of religion by giving us strong images for contemplation, for reflecting on the life-defining mysteries, and for educating ourselves so we can live them out more creatively.

—THOMAS MOORE

I deeply appreciate the idea of religion as a means to relate to the mysteries that define and give meaning to our lives. I imagine that many readers of this book have had struggles with the institutional church and some may even have stepped outside of the traditional borders. Yet our call as monks and artists is rooted in this rich monastic tradition of stories and practices that have persisted over hundreds of years. An icon artist I know once described her work as "serving the mysteries." I was entranced by that image, because for me the spiritual and creative journeys are not so much about growing in certainty—in many ways it is about growing less certain—as they are about learning how to move more deeply into the heart of mystery, into the great unknowing.

Instead of thinking our way through everything, we discover a deeper wisdom that emerges when we surrender to that which we can't articulate. Later in this book, the practices of humility and conversion will support us in this work. Our call as monks and artists is ultimately about serving the great mysteries of life and honoring this as a rich and fertile path.

Contemplative Practices

Invitation

This week you are invited to begin contemplating your own inner monk and artist. With which of these do you feel more resonance? What are the challenges you anticipate and the grace you hope to receive by getting to know them more deeply?

Lectio Divina

Allow your practice of lectio to be a time of slowing yourself down and being fully present to the invitations present in this moment. Lean into a sense of awe and wonder, of living at the edges of life and embracing holy mystery. Below is a suggested scripture passage for prayer this week:

> *Thus says the Lord:*
> *stand at the crossroads and look,*
> *and ask for ancient paths:*
> *where the good way lies; and walk in it,*
> *and find rest for your souls.*
>
> —JEREMIAH 6:16

This is a rich passage to pray with while walking. Consider printing it on a small slip of paper and read it over a couple of times, allowing a word or phrase to emerge for you. Then take this word or phrase on your walk with you, listening for the way it wants to unfold in your heart and the way the world around you is responding as well. After a while, pause and read the passage again and continue walking while listening for the invitation at this moment in your life. After spending some time with the way you are being invited to respond, move into contemplative silence while walking—release the words in your heart and move into being present to the world around you and to God's presence there. Rest in gratitude simply for the gift of being.

Reflection Questions

> *I regard monks and poets as the best degenerates in America. Both have a finely developed sense of the sacred potential in all things; both value image and symbol over utilitarian purpose or the bottom line; they recognize the transformative power hiding in the simplest things, and it leads them to commit absurd acts: the poem! the prayer! what nonsense! In a culture that excels at creating artificial, tightly controlled environments (shopping*

*malls, amusement parks, chain motels), the art
of monks and poets is use-less, if not irrespon-
sible, remaining out of reach of commercial
manipulation and ideological justification.*

—KATHLEEN NORRIS

- What if you cared less about achievements and being useful, and did more "useless" things?
- What would it mean for you to dance, make art, write poetry, and pray purely for the delight in the act of creation?
- What are the "degenerate" activities that call out to your heart? Consider engaging in one today.
- Where are the places and practices in your life where the way of the monk and the path of the artist merge? Where do they challenge one another?
- Where are the border spaces in your own life that invite you to linger? Will you respond to the call?

Visual Art Exploration

Wisdom Cards

Materials needed: three medium-sized rectangle-shaped pieces of watercolor paper (about 5"x 7"), watercolors (an inexpensive set is just fine), brush, jar of water, collage images (can be any inspiring image from a magazine, nature book, etc.), glue stick, pen, scissors, and roll of drafting tape. (Low tack tape is used for holding down paper—you could also use masking or painter's tape. Just apply it first to a piece of clothing and then remove to create some fuzz on the surface and reduce the stickiness so it doesn't tear the paper.)

1. Read through the exercise to make sure you understand the sequence and gather all of the materials needed. Allow yourself an hour or more to move through this process and let it be both a playful and prayerful experience.

Begin with some meditation. This could be gentle breathing or perhaps practicing lectio divina with the passage for this week, allowing yourself to sink more deeply into the embrace of God.

In *Letters to a Young Poet*, Rainer Maria Rilke writes, "Have patience with everything unresolved in your heart and try to love the questions themselves. . . . Live the questions now." Part of our call as monks and artists is to live and love the questions of our lives, the unresolved places. The arts help us to dwell in that space of the question by allowing us to honor the images and feelings without having to move to linear and logical thinking, the thinking that wants to find answers. Soul questions are those that speak to the deepest desires of our heart. They ask in different ways, "How am I seeking to create a meaningful life?" Phil Cousineau writes in *The Art of Pilgrimage* that "the purpose behind questions is to initiate the quest."

2. Take some time in silence to reflect on what *soul question* you want to ask of your inner monk, your inner artist, and of both of them together (three questions altogether). These questions will initiate your inner quest through art. Write down one of each of these soul questions on the back of each piece of paper. (You should have three different questions and three pieces of paper.) Then shuffle the papers so you don't know which paper holds which question on the reverse. As you move into the visual-expression experience, let the questions go for the time being.

3. Take a roll of tape. With the tape, create a frame around the edges of each piece of paper to hold them down to the table or work surface. Overlapping the edges of the paper will create a border after you paint.

4. Begin by taking some watercolors, brush, and small container of water and dip your brush in the water first, then the watercolors. Explore colors you feel drawn to and cover the background surface. Try to release your analytical mind and return to your breath as an anchor in the present moment.

5. After a time of painting, shift your attention to the collage images. As you sort through images, notice especially the ones that have resonance—a strong positive energetic draw—and the ones that have dissonance—a strong negative energetic resistance. Select the images that stir this inner movement, without making judgments about whether they are the "right" ones. Gather images through which you experience resonance or dissonance, and create collages for each of the three cards,

leaving as much of the painted background exposed as you would like. Keep returning to your breath as a way to stay grounded in the present moment, allowing your intuition to guide the process of placing the images in relationship to one another. Notice what happens internally during the process.

6. When the three pieces are done, do not turn them over just yet. Take some time to reflect on the process of creating each card:

- What did you notice in yourself? What were the voices and judgments that arose?
- Which of the collages felt the most freeing to create? Which one felt the most challenging?

7. After exploring the process for a time, take each image and turn it over to see which question corresponds with which card. Notice your own internal response as you discover what the synchronicity of images reveals about your question. Synchronicity sparks connections where we might not otherwise have seen them. See what wisdom the images have to offer to you. Take some time to journal about your discoveries. Consider inviting them to dialogue with one another to see what they have to say in conversation.

I encourage you to keep your wisdom cards somewhere visible. Continue to spend time with them throughout this journey and see what more they have to reveal. Creating art is like dreaming; there are a multitude of layers that can't be exhausted with just one sitting. Honor the art as an expression of your own soul and allow it to continue to reveal its meaning. The art and poetry you create each week will be a touchstone for you throughout this process.

Poetry Writing Exploration

I Am Going to Start Living Like a Mystic

Today I am pulling on a green wool sweater
and walking across the park in a dusky snowfall.
The trees stand like twenty-seven prophets in a field,
each a station in a pilgrimage–silent, pondering.
Blue flakes of light falling across their bodies
are the ciphers of a secret, an occultation.
I will examine their leaves as pages in a text
and consider the bookish pigeons, students of winter.
I will kneel on the track of a vanquished squirrel
and stare into a blank pond for the figure of Sophia.
I shall begin scouring the sky for signs
as if my whole future were constellated upon it.
I will walk home alone with the deep alone,
a disciple of shadows, in praise of the mysteries.

—EDWARD HIRSCH

One of my favorite poetry-writing prompts is to take the title of a poem I love and use it as the starting point for my own poem. The Edward Hirsch poem above speaks to what it means to live as mystic, artist, and monk in the world.

I invite you this week to write a poem with two or three parts. One part begins "I am going to start living like a monk," and the other part begins "I am going to start living like an artist." You might want to add a third part that begins "I am going to start living like a mystic" (or whatever word you might be inspired to engage).

Begin with some time to center yourself. Because poetry is rhythmic, slowing down and getting in touch with the rhythm of your breath is a great entry into writing poetry. Then take each beginning line as a prompt for writing, and free-write for several minutes on each topic. Write without editing yourself; allow the words to flow onto the page. If an image arises that feels odd, or you notice a judgment about whether it is the "right" image, simply notice that judgment with compassion and curiosity and release that voice and return to writing. Stay engaged with sense-specific images — what does being a monk or artist look like, smell like, taste like, sound like, and feel like? What does your instinct tell you about being a monk or artist?

After writing about each topic for several minutes, spend some time crafting the words into a poem and notice what is revealed to you through the experience.

> *Today, Lord, I come with clenched fist, locked jaw*
> *and a well used armory of weapons uselessly launched*
> *against all manner of enemy*
> *My list-making, crisis thwarting, horn-blasting attempts at hiding*
> > *from you*
> *I now determine to lay at your feet*
> *I will breathe into my shivering, fear frozen and gasping hesitancy*
> *This time Lord I loosen my grip and wait to hear your beckoning*
> *Pull me Lord through the fire of my human "doingness"*
> *Sit me midst my pain, my groaning I trust you'll hear.*
> *Lord gentle me into your silence*
> *Teach me to see into the depths of quiet pools*
> *Untangle my webs of clutter and chaos*
> *Awaken the monk in me*
> *Help me find the way back to my heart*
> *Today I am going to start living like an artist again*
> *Abandoning all that keeps me from believing*
> *That in this place, artist and monk alike*
> *are tuned to the rhythm of a thousand heartbeats*
> *And once again my wild gypsy dancing, now spirit soaring heart*
> *will sprout wings and take flight*
> *And all the angels will sing, for today— "she flew!"*
> > —LAURIE KATHLEEN CLARK

SACRED TOOLS *and* SACRED SPACE

Be. Here. This moment. Now is all there is, don't go seeking another. Discover the sacred in your artist's tools; they are the vessels of the altar of your own unfolding. Look at this cup of holy water, washing clean the brushes. See the blank page, awaiting your blessing. Gaze on the colors before you, each one a name of God: Saffron, Cobalt, Azure, Ruby. Say each one slowly and taste its juice in your mouth. Let this be your prayer. Brush them across the page. First the small strokes, then the larger sweeps. Lose track of all time. This too is prayer. Listen for the words that rise up: Awaken. Envision. Sing. Alleluia. Place marks on the page saying I am here. Watch as word and image dance together. Luminous. Illuminated. This is your sacred text. This is where God's words are spoken, sometimes in whispers, sometimes in shouts. Be there to catch them as they pass over those sacred lips, tumbling so generously into your open arms.

—Christine Valters Paintner

Sacraments of Daily Life

Let him regard all the utensils of the monastery
and its whole property as if they were the sacred vessels of the altar.

—*Rule of St. Benedict*

Now is the time to remember that all you do is sacred.

—Hafiz

One fruit of contemplation is that we slowly become more conscious of everything as a sacred vessel; each person and object, each moment in time is a dwelling place for the Holy Presence. When we are rushing through our days it is easy to forget this and so we *practice* presence and paying attention. One of my favorite lines from the whole of the *Rule of St. Benedict* is the one quoted above. It is a remarkable invitation to consider that everything—including every fork and spoon and spatula—is as sacred as the chalice on the altar. In fact, the kitchen table is the altar of daily nourishment, offering strength for your work in the world. Your art studio or writing desk is the altar of your creative heart, creating space for you to express the beauty arising within. When we are rushing through our days, it is easy to forget this and so we *practice* presence and paying attention.

This is one of the elements I love most about Benedictine spirituality. The cup you take down from your cupboard each morning for tea or coffee is as sacred as the chalice that holds the consecrated wine. St. Teresa of Avila, the great Carmelite mystic, said to the sisters of her community: "The Lord walks among the pots and pans." We make artificial divisions between sacred and secular, between what is worthy of our awe and gratitude and what is not. Esther de Waal writes that Benedictine life "simply consists in doing the ordinary things of daily life carefully and lovingly, with the attention and reverence that can make of them a way of prayers, a way to God."

The focus this week is to become more conscious of the ways everyday acts and objects are inherently sacred when performed and regarded with intention. When we focus on whatever we are doing, we discover that God is in the midst of our work. As artists and writers, we are invited to begin considering our tools as sacred implements. Brush and paint, paper and pen, are vessels of holiness.

The Sacred Art of Living

*The genius of Benedictinism is its concentration on living the active life contemplatively. Benedictine spirituality brings depth and focus to dailiness. Benedictine spirituality is as concerned with the way a thing is done as it is with what is done: guests are to be received as Christ (*RB *[Rule of Benedict] 53); foods are to be selected with care (*RB 39*); the goods of the monastery are to be treated reverently (*RB 32*); pilgrims and the poor are to be treated with special attention (*RB 66*)—all for the love of Christ. Life is not divided into parts holy and mundane in the Rule of Benedict. All of life is sacred. All of life is holy. **All of life is to be held in anointed hands** [emphasis added].*

—JOAN CHITTISTER

The regular practice of art making helps us to cultivate creative ways of being in the world. Ultimately, our greatest creative act is living our daily lives. Creativity is about making space; it is about listening to ourselves and to the world around us. We must see beyond the surface to the multiple dimensions of the world, opening ourselves to the newness that stirs there. We can cultivate a sense of spontaneity and playfulness, while honoring our commitments lovingly and intentionally.

Every aspect of our lives can be an arena for creative work. When we make space to breathe deeply—in our jobs, relationships, and leisure— we open ourselves up to give voice to vision and birth to newness. Creativity is an essential and life-giving practice that requires spaciousness, attention, and intention in order to flourish. As well, it requires a degree of surrender of our control over the process. It also requires listening to the wisdom of our intuition, our bodies, and our feelings while acknowledging that nourishing our creativity is a lifelong journey and process. We also need a community that helps us to discern the creativity that is waiting to be born into our lives.

What if we were to hold all of life with the anointed hands about which Chittister writes? Rise each morning and give thanks for the coffee that awakens our mind and body, offer gratitude for sleep and the renewal that comes with rest. Welcome in the morning each object that acts as a sacred vessel, supporting our own unfolding. As we eat breakfast, give thanks for each morsel of food and its source, offer praise for the gift of awakening; invite gratitude for the dishes on the counter and for the birdsong outside the window to swell our hearts. Consider turning your morning routine into a ritual of thanksgiving. Anoint your hands as the vessels of grace. As you touch each thing, let your skin offer its blessing.

What if, with each bite of food, we exclaimed in wonder at the ways our bodies take in nourishment and transform it into energy for our work and service in the world? Savoring oatmeal can become an act of praise. And as we read the morning news, what if we each took a moment to gather all the sorrow of the world into our hearts and held it there with great love and kindness so that we might carry this awareness to all those we encounter during our day? What if each drop of water that flows from our faucets reminded us of cleansing and the new birth that is possible in each moment? Could we walk along our path each day and find joy in the footprints and other offerings left by those who have traveled this path before us?

Our call as artists of everyday life is to consecrate the daily with our attention and awareness and then to bring this holy intimacy with the details of life to the process of creating.

> Sometimes when people ask me about my prayer life, I describe hanging laundry on the line. After a day of too much information about almost everything, there is such blessed relief in the weight of wet clothes, causing the wicker basket to creak as I carry it out to the clothesline. Every time I bend down to shake loose a piece of laundry, I smell the grass. I smell the sun. Above all, I smell clean laundry. This

> is something concrete that I have accomplished, a rarity in
> my brainy life of largely abstract accomplishments. . . .
>
> I hang each T-shirt like a prayer flag, shaking it first to get the
> wrinkles out and then pinning it to the line with two wooden
> clothespins. Even the clothespins give me pleasure. I add
> a prayer for the trees from which these clothespins came,
> along with the Penley Corporation of West Paris, Maine,
> which is still willing to make them from wood instead of
> colored plastic. (Barbara Brown Taylor)

Much of my own days are spent in a "brainy life of largely abstract
accomplishments." What Taylor describes here reminds me of my experience of walking as a way of grounding myself in the midst of much thinking. It brings me back to my body. I take pleasure in movement, in the feel
of my heart beating strongly, breathing air after a rainfall. Take a walk
this week and bring your full awareness to the experience; allow each
moment to bring you pleasure; let each step be a prayer. Hang a piece of
laundry and see it become a prayer flag before your eyes.

Contemplative Practices

Invitation

This week's invitation is to regard everything in your life as sacred,
including the tools you engage for your art making and writing and to
sanctify the space in which you work. It doesn't mean you have to buy
all new things or the most expensive supplies—far from it. We can be
seduced into thinking that buying stuff will be the answer. Then, once we
have all those beautiful objects around us, we are afraid to touch them
because what we create or write might not be perfect. The very stuff of
your daily life is already sacred.

Practice by bringing a sense of reverence to everything you do—both
those things that naturally call forth a sense of holy presence and those
things that you perhaps dread or do with a sense of drudgery. How might

your relationship to the tasks of daily life be transformed through this monastic vision?

Lectio Divina

This week for your lectio divina practice, I suggest praying with the words of this poem by Pablo Neruda. The process is the same as with scripture. Lectio divina invites us to expand our awareness and to discover the world around us as a sacred text, rich with the word of God.

> ### An Ode for Ironing
> *Poetry is white*
> *it comes dripping out of the water*
> *it gets wrinkled and piles up*
> *We have to stretch out the skin of this planet*
> *We have to iron the sea in its whiteness*
> *The hands go on and on*
> *and so things are made*
> *the hands make the world every day*
> *fire unites with steel*
> *linen, canvas and calico come back*
> *from combat in the laundry*
> *and from the light a dove is born*
> *purity comes back from the soap suds.*
>
> —PABLO NERUDA

Reflection Questions

- As artists and writers, you may already regard your work as a spiritual practice, but do you engage your tools as holy objects? Do you regard each implement as a sacred vessel on the altar of your transformation? What might happen if you made this an intentional part of beginning your work?
- When you lift your pen or brush, do you have a sense of the transformative potential this moment offers?
- How might you begin each day with an act of anointing your hands for holy service?

Visual Art Exploration

Creating a Personal Art Altar

I have two primary altar spaces in my home. One is in the prayer corner in our living room. It is set on top of a beautiful old secretary desk that is from my father's family. In the last century and a half, it has traveled from Latvia to Vienna to New York to Sacramento to San Francisco to Berkeley to Seattle. There is a secret compartment inside, and when I first lifted it open, I discovered a shipping document that had the seal of the Third Reich on it. Inside the desk I keep my journal and the many books I am reading. (I tend to read several at once, picking one up and then putting it down to ponder awhile.) On the altar itself are a variety of objects that have meaning for me—some stay permanently, like the triptych I had created by another artist to honor the importance of animal wisdom in my life, or the photo of my mother who died seven years ago.

Then there are the more temporary objects gracing this altar space, which usually reflect the season we are in, both liturgical and natural. I bring in a purple cloth for advent or some fallen leaves for autumn, a stone or leaf I found while walking, a small vase of spring flowers or a basket of hand-painted wooden eggs for Easter. There are other objects that live there to represent a phase from my life, such as a symbol for a particular transition I am experiencing. I also prop up art pieces that I have created myself from that place of prayer, giving them visual space to continue to have their meaning ripen in me. There is a tension here between those things that feel more permanent and enduring and those that are more fleeting, representative of my pilgrimage through time and its changing qualities.

Every so often, when I feel something new emerging in me, I clear off some space, take the objects that have been there and place them ever so carefully in the drawer below. I thank them for their wisdom and guidance so far, and leave space to listen for what new symbols want to dwell there and help reveal to me the next layer that needs tending. As I add new things that feel sacred, I slowly unfold my story.

The other altar I have is in my office, which functions as my writing and art studio. I have several bookshelves in this room lined with art supplies and pens and paper. One of the shelves holds several sacred objects that honor my creative power and encourage the holy spark to burn within me. This altar is more focused on objects that make me conscious of the sacred act of creating. Often I will use symbols of each of the four elements. For instance, I may include a feather (air) reminding me to take myself lightly, a candle (fire) encouraging the creative passions burning within me, a bowl (water) reminding me to follow the flow, and a stone (earth) symbolizing the ways my nature and my body ground me in the deep creative rhythms of the world.

Altars can be very powerful. In creating altars, we fill a personal space with the power of our own intentions and longings. We take seriously the deep desires of our hearts that St. Ignatius of Loyola wisely said were planted there by God in the first place. We acknowledge an incarnate God who speaks through symbols and the things of our everyday lives, and responds to our longings.

A personal altar is a sacred space where we can re-center and reconnect with the Holy Presence dwelling in our midst—a place to honor the desires of our lives with beauty. Altars help give voice to the longings bubbling up within us, long before we can put them into words. It is an act of trust and wisdom to listen to those symbols that want a place in our lives. It is a reminder that there is something greater, bigger than our daily worries and concerns.

- What are the sacred spaces in your home?
- Where are the places that you have intentionally devoted to reminding you of the presence of the holy?
- What are the symbols you have on your altar or the ones you would like to put on one?
- What longings need symbolic expression in your life right now?

For your visual art exploration this week, I invite you to create an altar space dedicated to honoring your life as an artist and writer. This might be just a small shelf or windowsill in your home near where you engage in your creative work. Even the corner of a table will do. Begin simply with a candle and a stone. Or you might gather several meaningful symbols—small statues, natural objects, or cloth—and create a larger altar if you have space. Allow its shape to emerge over the week and even

over the length of this course. Listen for the symbols that would be meaningful to you for this season ahead.

Poetry Writing Exploration

Writing a Blessing for Beginning Creative Work

I invite you this week to write a blessing to read as you begin any
creative project. What follows is a sample blessing written by Macrina
Wiederkehr. Make the blessing entirely your own, or take a line from
Wiederkehr as a starting place if you feel stuck. As you sit down to write,
paint, or draw, consider the ways you want to bless this work. What
awareness about how God is working through you do you want to bring
to this time? What do you need to remind yourself about the sacred tools
of your creative altar? A blessing helps us to shift our intention so that we
become aware that the time ahead is sacred. When we bless something we
give thanks while honoring the abundance that already exists.

In Jewish tradition, there are blessings for most activities of the day
as a way of consecrating each action. Blessings allow us to bring our
awareness to everything we do as a participation in the unfolding of the
sacred mystery in our daily lives. If you find writing the blessing for your
creative work satisfying, consider writing short blessings for other daily
tasks like cooking, sleeping, and cleaning.

Blessing Prayer to Begin a Creative Work

Materials needed: desk, pencils, pens, writing pads, computer, crayons, paints, and brushes—any tools serving you are to be anointed with a
look of love, a touch of the hand, a tender word, a breath of inspiration,
with oils or water . . . Whatever the soul calls you to do: obey.

I call on the angels:

O Gabriel, messenger of God—assist me in believing that
I have the potential to lift good news out of my soul that
I may be a messenger of beauty for my household and
beyond . . .

O Raphael, healing touch of God—heal the trepidation that prevents me from honoring my own creative spirit . . .

O Michael, strength of God—build up strength within me that I may rise to the challenge of being obedient to my creativity . . .

"Every blade of grass has its angel that bends over it and whispers . . . grow, grow." (The Talmud)

O Guardian angels everywhere—awaken in me that which is ready to be born this day . . . send forth all within me that is ready for wings.

I call in the saints and muses: Hildegard, Francis, Teresa of Avila, Benedict and Scholastica, Thomas Merton, Ernest Larkin, Mother Teresa, Catherine of Siena, Oscar Romero, Mechthild, and Gertrude—robe me with your passion for truth and for seeking God.

Mary Oliver, William Stafford, David Whyte, David Steindl-Rast, Annie Dillard, May Sarton, Laurens van der Post—share with me your deep-seeing eyes.

Jesus, the Christ—christen me with love.

O Colors of Earth, anoint me and robe me with all the attributes I need for my life work: purple for wisdom, meditation, transformation, and spirituality; red for passion, energy and courage; blues and greens for calm restfulness, balance, healing, hope, serenity, and contemplation; golden yellows for optimism and joy, lucidity, compassion and illumination, and orange for animation, creativity and enthusiasm; black and white for death and life, power and innocence, mysticism and truth.

All of nature—send your mystical energy upon my work: rocks, precious stones, pebbles, air, wind, breezes, storms, earth, flowers, trees, plants, water, lakes, ponds, rivers, oceans, streams and brooks, fire, moon and stars, sun, volcanoes, bonfires, burning candles, quiet lights, and bright lights.

O Let everything that is good bless my work!
— MACRINA WIEDERKEHR

Here are two blessings written by participants in my classes:
Great Spirit of Creation
Bless what is given me to use,
Bless the dance of making,
Bless what is made.
From my mind, [place my hands on my head]
From my heart, [place my hands on my heart]
Through my hands, [turn my hands out, palms up]
It is good, I am grateful. [palms together, bow]
— CINDY READ

A Blessing Before Beginning
You who created the heavens and the earth,
You whose hands made tables and chairs
and utensils for use around the house,
You who inspire my creative energy and expression:
Direct my mind, my heart, and my hands to
Create only what speaks truth,
Shares more fully understanding, and
Strengthens acts of compassion.
To you who created me,
Gratias maximas tibi ago (Thank you very much).
— TED ZARAGOZA

SACRED RHYTHMS FOR
CREATIVE RENEWAL

A major obstacle to creativity is wanting to be
in the peak season of growth and generation at all times . . .
but if we see the soul's journey as cyclical, like the seasons . . .
then we can accept the reality
that periods of despair or fallowness are like winter
—a resting time that offers us a period of creative hibernation, purification,
and regeneration that prepares us for the births of spring.

—LINDA LEONARD

One of my passions is helping people reconnect with the wisdom of the seasons. Spring, summer, autumn, and winter each have particular gifts and invitations. Paying attention to the rhythms of the natural world helps us to recognize the places within us that call for blossoming, fruitfulness, releasing, and resting. My walking practice is largely my way of listening to the invitations of the world and the questions of each season. Linda Leonard's quotation serves as a potent reminder for us as artists, writers, and creators to appreciate winter for its contemplative wisdom. Fallow times, like the resting of a field between growing seasons, are necessary in the creative journey.

As a writer and an artist, one of the seasons' greatest gifts is this profound wisdom of cycles, how everything is continuously rising and falling. When we are in a dry spell we may panic because the words or inspiration seem absent, but often it is a dormant time, a winter time of the soul. At these times, we are called to rest, both inwardly and outwardly, allowing time for the seeds to sprout again.

One of my favorite books is *Music of Silence: A Sacred Journey through the Hours of the Day* by David Steindl-Rast, a Benedictine monk, and Sharon Lebell. When I first read this book several years ago, it transformed my relationship with the ancient monastic tradition of praying the Liturgy of the Hours. This poetic exploration invites us to tune ourselves to the wisdom each hour calls us to consider. I began to see the rise and fall of the day as a mirror of the rise and fall of the year. Dawn is parallel to spring—the time of awakening and new possibilities. Day corresponds with summer—the time of fullness and fruitfulness, the height of the day's warmth. Dusk is analogous with autumn—the time of releasing and surrendering, of becoming aware of the reality of endings. Dark (or night) resembles winter—the time of resting, dreaming, incubating, and restoring.

The hours of the day offer similar wisdom. From sleeping to waking and sleeping again, we are invited to acknowledge that there is a time for everything: a time for waking and rising and embracing the work of the day; a time for slumber, dreams, and renewal; a time for creating and restoring, for flowering forth into the world, and for retreating and nourishing ourselves.

In our culture of constant productivity, it is challenging to honor these natural rhythms, and we may begin to believe that our worth is determined by how much we can produce. Even our art may be affected as we judge ourselves by how many books, paintings, or workshops we can create. I sometimes wonder if all of the creativity books that have been published in recent years feed into this phenomenon. They offer valuable inspiration but forget to honor the entire rhythm of the creative process. Yet the winter periods will come, and we can expend lots of energy resisting them at every turn. Or, we can gently surrender to these periods of spiritual restoration while listening attentively for spring budding.

The invitation of our inner monk is to live in this counter-cultural way, to recognize the depth in stillness. Embracing our inner monk in part means we can perceive mental blocks and spiritual or artistic dryness as periods of uncertainty, of incubating, of trusting the seeds deep beneath the surface. We recognize the rhythms of nature as the rhythms of our own soul. We have cycles and seasons as artists also. The rise and fall of our creative energies are central to the artistic process. Embracing quiet periods, rather than resisting them, can lead us to more peacefulness and deeper expression in our art making.

We find this creative tension between the inner path of the monk and the outer path of the artist reflected in the mystical tradition, where there are typically two main ways to encounter the divine. The first is the *kataphatic* tradition, or "the way of images." This is the primary path our artistic work engages. It is a process of coming to know God through symbols, art, movement, song, sculpture, architecture, and drama. The *kataphatic* path honors the ways in which the sacred is revealed through the sensual dimension of this world. It is the expressive work of our inner artists.

The second, complementary path is the *apophatic* tradition, or "the way of unknowing." This is the path of contemplative prayer, of moving beyond image to an experience of the sheer presence of God. God is always beyond the words and symbols we use to try to understand the nature of the divine. The *apophatic* way honors the truth that the sacred is always more vast than the language and images we use for definition. It is the contemplative work of our inner monks.

These two paths are integral to our spiritual journey. As creatures that know the world sensually, we are lured by the physical world to an understanding of God's multidimensionality. We discover the sacred in color, shape, form, scent, touch, and taste. However, at some point we must also recognize that these experiences do not exhaust the fullness of the sacred, and so we are moved to wordless wonder. There is a necessary dialectic between the celebration of creativity as a path to God and the embrace of silence as a way of acknowledging the vastness of the sacred.

These creative cycles of rising and falling, of outward expression and inward contemplation, are reflected in the common phases of our lives. We can find them in the rising and setting of the sun, the weekly rhythms of work and Sabbath, the monthly waxing and waning of the moon, the annual change in seasons, and, of course, in the cycles of our own life stages of aging and seasons of work and relaxation. In this way, nature has much to teach us about honoring these rhythms in our own lives so that we can embrace the wisdom of both fruitfulness and fallowness.

Praying the Hours

The extent to which we are divorced from the complementary rhythms of restfulness and creativity is the extent to which we are cut off from patterns of well-being within ourselves and in our relationships. If we fail to establish regular practices of stillness and rest, our creativity will be either exhausted or shallow. Our countenance, instead of reflecting a vitality of fresh creative energy that is sustained by the restorative depths of stillness, will be listless or frenetic. This is as true collectively as it is individually, and applies as much to human creativity as it does to the earth's fruitfulness. Creativity without rest, and productivity without renewal, leads to an exhaustion of our inner resources.

—J. PHILIP NEWELL
THE BOOK OF CREATION

The ancient tradition of praying the Liturgy of the Hours, with its seven holy pauses, is at heart a communal prayer and a way of keeping conscious awareness of God's presence throughout the day. The Celtic monastic tradition offers us insight for becoming more present to the wisdom of the night and day. Celtic spirituality considers dawn and dusk to be "thin places" where heaven and earth are closer together.

Another gift of praying the Hours is the opportunity to grow in our awareness of the rhythms of the day, which correspond with the natural and liturgical seasons of the year, as well as the seasons of our lives. The Hours call us to become more deeply in touch with the central rhythm of waxing and waning. We can do so in many ways, including the flowering of spring and the release of autumn, the phases of the moon, and the movement from death to resurrection. The Hours teach us that waning in particular is an essential energy in our lives. We live in a culture of perpetual waxing, of striving to do as much as possible and squeeze as much as we can into a day. Yet nature offers us a very different way of being. As Newell says, creativity depends on the waning times for restoration as much as the times of work. How might your creative process be nourished by the simple act of allowing yourself some more spaciousness?

The same concept can be applied to the different periods of a day, which offer unique qualities to contemplate and new questions to ponder for our spiritual and artistic journeys. Creativity moves in cycles just as the earth does. We all have experienced the flow and ease of the time when we are immersed in a project and are feeling inspired. We lose track of time; we feel carried by something bigger than ourselves. Then there are the moments when we feel absolutely blocked. The well has run dry, and we are perhaps convinced that inspiration will never come again. Then we go for a walk or wash the dishes, and suddenly in the midst of that rhythm, when our mind has emptied, illumination enters again.

Psychologist Graham Wallas, in his work *Art of Thought*, published in 1926, was one of the first to present a model of the creative process. He identified three phases: preparation, incubation, illumination, and verification. These are not meant to be linear steps, but a circular movement where we might go back and forth between two of these or experience them in a different order.

I was initially captivated by the stage of incubation. I had experienced the movement from incubation to illumination many times in my life, but in reading Wallas's explanation, I suddenly connected that time of incubation to the rhythms of Sabbath each week and the longer rhythms of rest and renewal that come each year. I realized that releasing from my doing and entering fully into being, would always allow inspiration to visit me. The implications for this seem profound. In cultivating our creativity, times of rest are essential. Pushing ourselves to the edge of exhaustion does not nurture the creative process in the long run. Everything in creation goes through cycles of growth and decay. The artist's task is to remind humanity that we're part of a great family of being, that we are included in a cyclical process of companionship, disappearance, and reemergence.

> A people who farmed and knew the patterns of the seasons, who lived close to the sea and watched the ebb and flow of tides, above all who watched the daily cycle of the sun and the changing path of the moon, brought all of this into their prayer. Here is a way of praying that is essentially holistic. I am reminded that as a human being living on this earth I am a part of the pattern of day and night, darkness and light, the waxing and waning of the moon, the rising and setting

of the sun. The whole of myself is inserted into the rhythm of the elements and I can here learn something, if I am prepared to, of the ebb and flow of life itself. (Esther de Waal)

The monastic tradition of praying the hours of the day originated in Judaism. The practice of praying seven times a day is from the psalms: "Seven times a day I praise you" (Ps 119:164). The intention was to follow St. Paul's invitation to "pray without ceasing" (1 Thes 5:17) in an unending cascade of prayer.

Vigils: Night

To know the dark, go dark. Go without sight,
and find that the dark, too, blooms and sings.

—WENDELL BERRY

I love the dark hours of my being
in which my senses drop into the deep.

—RAINER MARIA RILKE

Vigils, also known as matins, is the first hour of the day, falling between midnight and dawn. Great wisdom can be found in the ways that the Christian and Jewish traditions begin the day with night. It is from the dark space of our mothers' wombs that we first emerge, and we will return to the body of the dark earth. The hidden hours of the night invite us to dwell in the darkness and see with a different kind of vision, to listen attentively to the music that emerges from the dark.

Vigil prayer is one of waiting, tending, listening, and surrendering to the wisdom of the night. We often hold a lot of fear around darkness, and yet the night invites us to a different way of being. We do not like to wait in a culture of instant gratification. Yet we are called to dwell in the dark, fertile soil of the earth, in that space where seeds incubate and begin their cycle of growth. Here we can cultivate a different way of seeing the possibilities not yet named and dreams being born. In nurturing creativity we must learn how to rest in periods of unknowing, finding peace in the knowledge that movement is happening far below the surface of what we can see.

Lauds: Dawn

Let us get up then, at long last, for the scriptures
rouse us when they say: It is high time for us to
arise from sleep (Rom 13:11).

—RULE OF ST. BENEDICT, PROLOGUE

The breezes at dawn have secrets to tell you, don't go back to sleep.

—RUMI

Lauds means "praise," and the hour of lauds is the hour of joy and gratitude at the coming of the light—delight in a new day spread before us. We wake from the gift of rest, renewed and ready to enter a new day with all of its possibilities. Lauds is the beginning of another pilgrimage through the day ahead, our daily journey that offers gifts, challenges, and blessings unknown to us in this moment. We praise God for the world being reborn. It is the hour of resurrection, when we look to our own lives and what needs to be brought to life. It is the moment of the day parallel to our experience of inspiration, which means "to be breathed into."

David Whyte has a wonderful poem for morning called "What to Remember When Waking." In it he writes that "In that first hardly noticed moment in which you wake . . . there is a small opening into the new day / which closes the moment you begin your plans." The hour of lauds is the time that we are invited to welcome possibility and discovery. Recall the words of Isaiah from our lectio divina practice during the first week, and, as you wake, remember that God is creating something new in you this day—something of which you know nothing. You might consider creating a ritual for your morning in which you hold your plans lightly and anticipate the delight of discovery in the day ahead.

Terce: Morning

First of all, every time you begin a good work,
you must pray to him most earnestly to bring it
to perfection.

—RULE OF ST. BENEDICT, PROLOGUE

Work is love made visible.

—KAHLIL GIBRAN

Terce and the next two hours of the day are called the "little hours" because of their shorter and simpler liturgical structure. This is the morning time when our work is planned, assigned, and begun.

As a time of promise and possibility, morning is the occasion to reflect on how we shape and are shaped by our creative work, which is a primary way of expressing and giving form to the talents we have been given. Thus, our work becomes an offering to the world. Our offering shapes who we are by our daily engagement with it. Giving form to our creative ideas is about being seen and witnessed and entering into relationship with the world.

Sext: Noon

Be ablaze with enthusiasm. Let us be a live burn-
ing offering before the altar of God.

—HILDEGARD OF BINGEN

Why not become fire?

—DESERT FATHERS

Sext is the hour of midday when the sun is at its highest point in the sky. In the creative cycle, it is the hour of full illumination and the time when we experience the full joy of our work. Noon is the tilting point of the day when the light that has been expanding up to this moment will now begin its slow journey of contraction until we find ourselves in night again.

During this hour, the fire of the sun's heat is at its highest, and we are invited to reflect on the fire that burns within us. The morning was our time for beginnings; now we are invited to pause and make sense of our work and enter into the afternoon in ways that build upon the morning's energy.

None: Mid-afternoon

Teach us to count our days that we may gain a wise heart.

—PSALM 90:12

None is the mid-afternoon hour when shadows begin to lengthen. We are nearing the end of our workday and anticipate the rest that evening offers. We are invited in this hour to reflect on our own limitations. We may start to lose energy or lose focus on what we are doing.

In facing the reality of our own decline and eventual death, we may also discover the gift of being invited fully into each moment. Awareness of our mortality helps us to cherish life in all of its wonder and beauty. When you remember the fact that you will one day die, what are the creative dreams and longings that rise up with urgency within you?

Mid-afternoon is the time to bring our work to a strong finish, while holding the tension of knowing that everything in our work will also fade and disappear.

Vespers: Evening

When you turn around, starting here,
lift this New Glimpse that you found;
carry into evening all that you want from this day.

—WILLIAM STAFFORD

Vespers is the sacred hour when evening begins its descent. We put away the tools of our labor and we offer thanks for the gifts of the day and forgiveness for its hurts. Evening invites us to enter into stillness, to ponder the paradox of the day's rise and fall and our own simultaneous fruitfulness and dying. We are asked to cease "doing" and start simply "being." We might do this by gathering with friends and family to share in some sacred nourishment and conversation.

Sunsets offer a glorious celebration of our waning time, much like autumn announces the beauty of death in vibrant color. In Celtic tradition, dusk or twilight is considered to be a "thin place" where the veil between heaven and earth is lifted and we can more easily see the sacred. In the creative process, it is the time of releasing the work of doing and allowing our being to nourish our vision. We remember that the work is not entirely ours, but is supported by a greater source.

Compline: Night

No matter how deeply I go down into myself
my God is dark, and like a webbing made
of a hundred roots that drink in silence.

—RAINER MARIA RILKE

The night will give you a horizon wider than you can see.

—DAVID WHYTE

The hour of compline brings us back full circle to the darkness. We are invited in this moment to reenter the gift of rest and renewal. Our only light is the illumination we reach out for—perhaps a candle, a lamp, or the glowing flame in the heart of our beloved.

In many monastic communities, compline is the moment of entering into the great silence, the invitation to let go of speech for the evening and allow oneself to be bathed in another language that emerges from the space of darkness. This is a sacred language that speaks to us of holy possibility, of creativity emerging from the vast pool of night.

Widening Circles

I live my life in widening circles
that reach out across the world.

—Rainer Maria Rilke

Round and round the earth is turning
Turning always round to morning
And from morning round to night.

—Anonymous

The Liturgy of the Hours calls us back to pray at regular intervals, to recognize the different invitations the day offers to us, and to remind ourselves that the center of our lives is God and not our work. Most of us live in artificial rhythms ruled by the demands of the marketplace. We can become enslaved by our drive for more productivity and possessions. Thomas Merton wrote: "The whole world runs by rhythms I have not yet learned to recognize, rhythms that are not those of the engineer." In a technological world, we live by engineered rhythms, rhythms that demand we are "on" and accessible most hours of the day.

As a monk and artist, I want to rise and fall like the ebb and flow of the ocean. I want to shed parts of myself in autumn, to go deeply inward in winter, to blossom into spring, and to shine forth and be radiant in summer. I want to live my life in healing rhythms that honor the limits of my body, the pleasures of rest, and the delights of play.

I want to live my life in awareness of its widening circles:

- Each day, the turning of the earth, the rising and setting of the sun, honoring the varying qualities and gifts of light and darkness . . .
- Each week, a day of Sabbath rest when I release the world's hold on me . . .
- Every four weeks, the moon moving through her cycle, growing into fullness, before her gentle waning until she disappears for a night into blackness . . .
- Every four months, the turning of the seasons and the slow movement to a new way of being in the world . . .
- Each year, remembering the day of my birth and the births of all those I love. I give special honor to the commitment of my marriage, the renewal of my commitment as an oblate, and the days that recall the great losses in my life.
- Every seven years, the changing of each cell in the body, and we are made completely new . . . Then there is the largest personal cycle—
- A lifetime. My own life will fall into the great beyond, a rhythm that is not predictable nor solid like the turning of the earth. I am only sure it will happen and I give myself to it. In that giving I receive a life filled with blessing.

Contemplative Practices

Invitation

Focus on paying attention to your own inner rhythms. This involves paying attention to the way your energy rises and falls naturally throughout the day, as well as embracing the outer rhythms of nature in a day, in lunar cycles, and in natural seasons. Notice any particular ways you would like to honor those rhythms through incorporating morning and evening prayer into your routine, keeping a Sabbath day, or taking a retreat. Carve out some time to be present to these rhythms in more intentional ways. How might bringing purpose and awareness to these rhythms nurture your creative expression?

Lectio Divina

For your lectio divina practice, I suggest the following scripture from Ecclesiastes — one you have probably heard many times. But as often happens with words repeated frequently, they lose their impact and deserve a fresh look. So as you read and pray, I invite you to really rest into the wisdom offered here, allowing yourself to savor each word and to listen for your invitation:

> *For everything there is a season, and a time for every matter under*
> *   heaven:*
> *a time to be born, and a time to die;*
> *a time to plant, and a time to pluck up what is planted;*
> *a time to kill, and a time to heal;*
> *a time to break down, and a time to build up;*
> *a time to weep, and a time to laugh;*
> *a time to mourn, and a time to dance;*
> *a time to throw away stones, and a time to gather stones together;*
> *a time to embrace, and a time to refrain from embracing;*
> *a time to seek, and a time to lose;*
> *a time to keep, and a time to throw away;*
> *a time to tear, and a time to sew;*
> *a time to keep silence, and a time to speak;*
> *a time to love, and a time to hate;*
> *a time for war, and a time for peace.*
> *   —*ECCLESIASTES 3:1–8

Reflection Questions

- Which internal season are you in right now? What is it time for in your life?
- How might you begin to honor the daily, weekly, monthly, and annual rhythms of nature? How can these rhythms support your life as an artist and monk?
- When you enter a fallow period, are you able to offer room for your soul to truly rest and renew?
- In this season, are you being called to renew yourself or to extend your gifts into this world?

Meditation: Seasons of the Breath

The hour of dawn is associated with the direction of the east and with springtime. It is the hour of awakening, blossoming, and newness. Dawn is the time of day when everything seems possible. In Cherokee tradition, the element of air is connected to dawn and spring, as dawn is the moment when we breathe in our first breath of the day and awaken to ourselves again. Our breath can also teach us about this season—the experience of inhalation is the moment of in-breathing the gift of life. Consider placing a feather on your altar in the direction of the east to honor the element of air.

Noon is associated with the season of summer as well as the direction of the south in the Northern Hemisphere and north in the Southern Hemisphere. It is the hour of fullness and the height of the sun's illumination. Midday is the time that we are fully immersed in our work in the world. In Cherokee tradition, the element of fire is connected to day and summer, as noon is the height of the day's heat. The moment between inhaling and exhaling offers us an experience of this fullness within us. Consider placing a candle on your altar in the corresponding direction (toward the south if you are in the northern hemisphere and north if you are in the southern hemisphere) to honor the element of fire.

The hour of dusk is associated with autumn and the direction of west. Dusk is the time we become aware of our limitations and endings. In Cherokee tradition, the element of water is connected to dusk and autumn, as we become conscious of the ebb and flow of our lives. When exhaling, we can experience the release and surrender of autumn and evening. We are reminded perhaps of the coming of our last breath. Consider placing a bowl of water on your altar in the direction of the west to honor the element of water.

The hour of dark (or night) is associated with the season of winter and the direction of north in the Northern Hemisphere and south in the Southern Hemisphere. It is the hour of stillness and rest, of moving inward as the days shorten. Dark is the time we are invited into deepest contemplation and uncertainty of everything that seemed so assured in the light of day. In Cherokee tradition, the element of earth is connected to dark and winter, as dark/winter is the moment of return to our roots, grounding, and the seeds that lie dormant deep within the soil. The moment between exhaling and inhaling is a place of vulnerability, of not knowing when the breath will come; it is a time of resting in stillness. Consider placing a stone on your altar toward the north if you are in the northern hemisphere and south if you are in the southern hemisphere to honor the element of earth.

This is a simple meditation of paying attention to the different qualities of breath. Begin by getting into a comfortable position and closing your eyes, if you would like. Start to pay attention to your breath, without changing anything. Simply take a few moments to connect with this life-sustaining energy moving through you.

Now begin to slow down your breath and move into an awareness of the four parts of breathing: there is the moment of inhaling, the pause between your inhaling and exhaling, the moment of exhaling, and the pause between your exhaling and inhaling. Aware of all four points, take a couple of breaths and notice the different qualities of each moment.

Let's explore each of these moments. To begin, as you breathe, focus on inhaling and allow your air intake to be slow and full. As you repeat each breath cycle, notice how that moment of breathing in—taking in oxygen—feels in your body. Call to mind the dawn as a time of awakening, an experience of breathing in new life. Experience spring blossoming in your body. Hold this question: how are you invited to awaken today? Take a few moments of silence to simply experience the fullness of your inhalation with each breath.

Now, as you continue noticing your breath, bring your focus to the moment between inhaling and exhaling. Pause for just a moment and notice how this moment of the breath feels in your body; experience the fullness of oxygen in your lungs. With each breath cycle, pause at this moment and focus on the height of the day as a time of fullness. Feel the experience of summer's heat and fruitfulness in your body. Hold this question: how are you invited into the fullness of who you are today? Take a few moments of silence to experience this moment between inhaling and exhaling.

Continue to notice your breath, but begin to focus on your exhalation and allow it to be slow and full. As you repeat each breath cycle, notice how that moment of breathing in feels in your body; sink into the experience of surrender and release that exhaling invites us into. With each breath you exhale, think of dusk as a time to let go, an experience of releasing that which no longer serves you, of being confronted with your own mortality and the knowledge that one day you will release your final breath. Feel the experience of autumn's vulnerability in your body. Hold this question: what are you invited to release today? Take a few moments of silence to experience the surrender of your exhalation with each breath.

Now we move to the final part of the breath. As you continue your breath cycles, bring your focus to the moment between exhalation and inhalation, and pause there for a moment with each breath. Experience the emptiness of the moment when breath leaves your body and you await the next breath you inhale. Allow yourself to rest for a moment in that place of discomfort and uncertainty. As you repeat each breath cycle, notice how that moment of breathing in feels in your body. Call to mind the night as a time of darkness and unknowing, a time of resting and waiting. Feel the experience of winter's call to rest in your body. Hold this question: how are you invited to be still today? Take a few moments of silence to simply experience this moment between exhaling and inhaling with each breath.

Now return to your normal breathing pattern and notice how your body is feeling. Take a few moments to see if you can become aware of the full cycle of your breath. Allow all four parts to have a moment of pause and awareness. Move through the seasons of spring, summer, autumn, and winter with each breath. Transition through the hours of the day with each breath. Experience the rise and fall in your body, knowing that this is the rhythm at the heart of creation as well.

I invite you to take just a few minutes each day in the week ahead to practice this breath awareness and see what it has to teach you.

You can also allow this practice to anchor you in an experience of the particular hour of the day you are in. So if you do this practice in the morning, rest in the experience of inhalation and awakening as a way to experience the full quality of this hour.

At each of these moments of the day, become aware of what the invitation is in that particular season and notice your own response.

Poetry Writing Exploration

Haiku for the Hours

Haiku is a simple and accessible poetic form. Writing three lines of five, seven, and five syllables respectively, focuses your attention and expresses the heart and essence of a particular moment. Haiku generally concern nature and the seasons, so I invite you to compose one or two haiku for each of the four main movements of the day—dawn, day, dusk, and dark—or one for each of the seven traditional hours. Pay attention to how the rise and fall of the day invites you into a particular awareness of your creative process. Consider including these haiku in your *Contemporary Book of Hours* (project following).

Visual Art Exploration

Contemporary Book of Hours

Materials needed: paper, watercolors, images, glue, brush.

The Book of Hours is a beautiful art form. Many were created in the Middle Ages as prayer books for wealthy lay people who wanted to have a resource from which they could pray the monastic hours in their everyday lives. The text was written in calligraphy and was accompanied by beautiful illustrations called illuminations because they helped to illuminate the meaning of the prayer in visual ways and because of the use of gold in the images. Sometimes when I am walking on a brilliant summer day and the world feels illuminated, I wonder if those ancient monks used gold in their books as a way to mirror the dazzling beauty of the sunlight.

I invite you this week to create your very own contemporary *Book of Hours*. Instead of copying the ancient psalms and prayers, and drawing elaborate designs to accompany them (although feel free to go in this direction if you would like), make a simple book form with your own poetry and words expressing the beauty of each hour of the day. You can explore all seven traditional hours of the monastic day—vigils (night), lauds (dawn), terce (morning), sext (noon), none (mid-afternoon), vespers (evening), and compline (night)—or just focus on the four primary movements of dawn, day, dusk, and dark.

For the visual element of your book, you might gather together images that remind you of the quality and gifts of a particular hour. You could also include your own photography or create simple collages from colored paper or paper you have painted with watercolor. If you are a fabric artist, feel free to include cloth and thread as your media. Each hour of the day has a certain quality of color and light, so you might try to express this through your choice of art medium.

To create your own book, I suggest you use an accordion book structure. You can do a Web search for "accordion book" and several simple instructions will come up. You can create an accordion out of a single long piece of paper by folding it back and forth upon itself so it looks like one long accordion. An alternative is to take multiple sheets of paper and fold each one in half. Overlap the pages so they create an accordion, and glue the pages together where the insides meet.

Participants in my online course have created this book from paper and paint (watercolor or acrylic), collage images, fabric and embroidery, and their own photographs. Listen for what medium feels most resonant for you with this project to express the sacred seasons of the day.

> *Glorious God wake*
> *me with your Love and Fury*
> *Shield me in your gold*
>
> —LYNN PENNEY
>
> *eastern sky reveals*
> *deeply tinted air; inhale*
> *welcome the new day*
>
> —ANNE BUCK
>
> *fullness of day's breath*
> *brings forth energy of creation*
> *hold the momentum*
>
> —EVELINE MAEDEL

Beautiful cycle
Of sun's radiant love
Transforms seed to flower

—CHERYL MACPHERSON

Thank you for today.
Did I live free and bring peace?
I kneel and know joy.

—JUDY SMOOT

Moon beautiful moon
Ripe-fruited night sky Goddess
Gracefully waning

—YVONNE LUCIA

OBEDIENCE, STABILITY, CONVERSION: COMMITMENT *to the* CREATIVE LIFE

When a monk joins a Benedictine community and enters the monastery, he promises to live according to the Benedictine way of life. Three commitments essential to this way of life are obedience, stability, and conversion. Each is countercultural and challenging to the status quo—the way we usually go about our lives. What do these responsibilities mean in light of our creative commitments, and how do they support our lives outside of a monastic community? We will explore each one in this chapter and consider how to integrate their meaning into our lives.

Obedience

Here is one thing in this world that you must never forget to do. If you forget everything else and not this, there's nothing to worry about; but if you remember everything else and forget this, then you will have done nothing in your life. It's as if a king has sent you to some country to do a task, and you perform a hundred other services, but not the

one he sent you to do. So human beings come to this world
to do particular work. That work is the purpose, and each is
specific to the person. If you don't do it, it's as if a priceless
Indian sword were used to slice rotten meat. It's a golden
bowl being used to cook turnips, when one filing from the
bowl could buy a hundred suitable pots. . . . *Remember the
deep root of your being, the presence of the only Being.
Give your life to the one who already owns your breath and
your moments.*

—RUMI

The word "obedience" comes from the root word *audire,* meaning "to
hear." Obedience is about listening deeply to the ways God calls you in
everyday life and how you respond. Listening is not an activity so much
as an invitation to intimacy. Rumi's words express the poetic dimension
of obedience—of being faithful to the task to which you are called and
not spending your precious life energy on what doesn't further that call.
Obedience is a commitment to hearing the sacred whispers summoning
you forward into your unique call each moment of the day and your full-
hearted "yes" to that call. In light of creativity, obedience challenges us to
listen and be present to the way God whispers to us through our creative
process, and to respond to the invitations we hear. We make space for
silence in our lives so that we might be able to hear more clearly.

Recall the scripture passage from Isaiah in week one. Remember
how God creates a new thing this very moment, something that cannot be
anticipated. Obedience for me is something like this: listening for the way
life is calling, beyond what I can imagine for myself, and then responding to that invitation. This requires taking a step, a leap, without prepar-
ing. Obedience means trusting that I was created as a creative being in
the image of the Primary Creator and realizing that what brings me joy
and energy will also bring me closer to my purpose. How are you being
invited to listen more closely to the call of your life? What would it mean
to respond to that call wholeheartedly? How does the vow of obedience
illumine your commitment to the way of the monk and the path of the
artist?

When you remember the "deep root of your being," what does it
mean to be obedient to the call of your inner monk and inner artist?

Stability

Stability is perceived as an antidote to the restlessness of mind and heart in which a person searches for new experiences, new relationships, and new geographical locations to escape difficulties or to solve problems by avoiding them. This unceasing search for the new and extravagant, of course, can too often make life and relationships superficial, and any intimacy between people extremely fragile. Stability, however, can help a person stand still and listen, truly listen, as the Rule encourages one to do. It is similar to what the Quakers call "centering down" and Buddhists "mindfulness": the discipline of paying attention to "what is going on in the present moment," which can give rise "to insight, awakening, and love."

—Edward C. Sellner

Edward C. Sellner describes three qualities of stability in his book *Finding the Monk Within*: stability of place, stability of community, and stability of heart. Stability of place is the first layer of this vow. Monks in the Benedictine tradition make a commitment to live their entire lives in the monastery they join. The idea is that they do not run away from challenges and difficulties. It is similar to the commitment we make when we get married or begin other significant friendships—"for better or worse" means we stay and work to improve the relationship even when we want to run in the other direction.

I also think about stability of place as commitment to our local culture—getting to know our neighbors, learning the history and stories of the people who have dwelled on the land, honoring the rituals and practices woven into the landscape, discovering the names of wildlife and botanicals, becoming intimate with the place where we find ourselves. This is at the heart of finding the sacred everyday—discovering that the place where we are is enough, that God dwells right here, and we do not need to go anywhere else to find holiness. Stability of place invites us to enter into a kinship with the landscape. This helps form the matrix from which our creative work is expressed.

Similarly, stability of community asks for a lifetime commitment to a particular surrounding. Much like a layperson's commitment to family, friends, neighborhoods, and religious groups, monks commit to live in intentional communities. As artists and monks in the world living in border spaces, we might sometimes feel isolated from others who might understand our path. The call in this instance is to make a commitment to find kindred spirits and be present to the challenge of relationship. We will explore contemplative and creative communities a bit more in week eight.

Finally, there is stability of the heart. Esther de Waal writes that "the vow of stability is altogether fundamental, for it raises the whole issue of commitment and fidelity," which is so foreign to contemporary Western life. She reminds us that we cannot confront the basic questions of life without stability, and without stability we cannot come to know our true selves. Catherine de Hueck Doherty says, "You must understand that the *poustinia* (the Russian word for a place of solitude where one can communicate with God) begins in your heart. It is not a place, a geographical spot. It is not first and foremost a house or a room. It is within your heart." The *poustinia* is the inner monastery. Stability means not running away from yourself. When the creative work becomes challenging or the inner voices and judgments rise up, stability summons us to stay present to the process and see what we discover.

Where do you encounter restlessness in your contemplative and creative life? What are the moments when you are tempted to run in the other direction instead of standing still and being fully present to the gifts and challenges of the moment?

Conversion

Translations vary, but in our modern day, *conversatio morum suorum* generally means conversion of manners, a continuing and unsparing assessment and reassessment of one's self and what is most important and valuable in life. In essence, the individual must continually ask: What is worth living for in this place at this time? And having asked, one must then seek to act in accordance with the answer discerned.

—PAUL WILKES

Conversion is the counterpoint to stability. Held in life-giving tension with the call to stay present is the call to always be growing and changing. In contemplative practice, the interior movement is to grow in our capacity for love: We expand our hearts to be able to welcome more into our loving gaze. Conversion begins with ourselves, as we cultivate compassion for our own desires and the choices we have made. Then we are gradually able to see those who were invisible to us and give them the dignity of our attention. As we grow in this capacity, we begin to encounter God in more places and experiences. We open ourselves to being surprised by God in the moments when our hearts previously would have been closed.

When we commit to conversion, we commit to a continual process of growth, of stumbling regularly and getting up again. We agree to potentially looking foolish because of our passions. In doing so, we discover that the greatest transformations happen when we are willing to step into the unknown space between our egos and our deepest longings. Conversion is central to creativity because it calls us to begin again and try new things.

Contemplative Practices

Invitation

Your invitation this week is to ponder the meaning of obedience, stability, and conversion for your own contemplative and creative practice. How do these commitments challenge you to think more deeply about what it means to be a monk and an artist in the world? Where do you experience resonance and dissonance with their invitations?

Lectio Divina

For your lectio divina practice this week, pray with this poem while reflecting on the grace and challenge of staying present in trying times — of staying open to the surprises awaiting you:

> **Life Is Calling**
> *A small investment in one step*
> *produces rich results*
> *Beyond what you can dream*
> *So shelve the hideaways*
> *the high performance*
> *the hardeners*
> *the penetrating grey*
> *And take on a whole new beautiful*
> *Turn ordinary works into*
> *an extraordinary existence*
> *Everything you need to turn*
> *slate blue into summer straw*
> *is here*
> *Welcome to safety — and adventure*
> *On a path that suits your*
> *specific needs*
> *In a way you can't imagine*
> *Life is calling*
> *To one step*
> *No preparation*
> *Just a leap of Faith*
> *So be transformed by the falling*
> *Start as who you think you are*
> *And find joyous, dancing water.*
>
> —KELLY MOORE

Reflection Questions

- What is your creative calling? How do you respond when you hear it?
- When you move into creative expression and fear rises up, do you stay or run? When resistance kicks in, do you listen to what it has to say to you, making space for its wisdom?
- In what ways do you allow God to surprise you?

Meditation and Movement Exploration

Hand Dance Blessing

> There is a vitality, a life force, an energy, a quick-
> ening that is translated through you into action,
> and because there is only one of you in all of
> time, this expression is unique. And if you block
> it, it will never exist through any other medium
> and it will be lost. The world will not have it. It
> is not your business to determine how good it
> is nor how valuable, nor how it compares with
> other expressions. It is your business to keep it
> yours clearly and directly, to keep the channel
> open. You do not even have to believe in your-
> self or your work. You have to keep yourself open
> and aware to the urges that motivate you. Keep
> the channel open.
>
> —MARTHA GRAHAM

This week we are trying something a little different. Instead of a visual art exploration, I invite you into a movement meditation from an improvisational practice called InterPlay®, which is a series of tools and practices developed by Cynthia Winton-Henry and Phil Porter for embodied exploration and playful discovery. This gentle meditation experience, a hand dance, involves putting on some music, closing your eyes, and dancing using just one hand. The exercise connects us to the wisdom of our bodies while we respond to the way our hand wants to move. This exercise allows us to enter into discovery and experience.

Begin with guided imagination and then movement exploration. You may choose to lie down on the ground or sit in a chair. You also need to select some music that is about three or four minutes long, and have it available for the time of movement. Perhaps you already have a piece that comes to mind. One song I choose for this exercise is "Blessing to the World" sung by Trish Bruxvoort Colligan of The River's Voice in the album *Splash* (www.RiversVoice.com).

Meditation: Hearts and Hands

1. Before you begin, take some time to center yourself, connect to your breath, and focus on your heart. Place your hand on your heart to make a physical connection. As you are mindful of your heart, imagine the spark of the divine, which according to the mystics, burns brightly there. Connect to this sacred dwelling place of the Holy One—your inner monastery or *poustinia*, the cave of your heart where God meets you with great joy. Begin to imagine back through time to the moment you were first created, shaped, and molded. Imagine that in this first moment of emerging from God's creative energies God blesses you with gifts for the world. You are bestowed with gifts that only you can give in your unique way, and your call in this life is to give them freely. Take a moment to notice the images that come to mind. What are the gifts God imprinted on your heart from the very beginning? Focus on these gifts, allowing images, feelings, and memories to rise up. Simply be present to them without trying to figure everything out. Rest for a while in this experience. Then in your imagination, allow for an energetic connection from your heart to your hands as a symbol of extending your gifts to the world. Hold your hands out and picture them as the way your heart meets the sacred presence in the world around you.

Movement Exploration: Hand Dance

2. With one hand in front, explore the space around you. Move your hand through the air in front of you. Try making smooth movements, then jerky ones. Then try smooth and slow, then jerky and fast. Create a shape with your hand, then another, then another. Explore the boundaries of the space around you, seeing how far your hand can reach. Rest your hand somewhere on your body and feel that physical connection. Then rest your hand somewhere else and pause.

Play the song you have selected for this time. Allow this to be a time of moving meditation and discovery. Trust this process and try not to think it through. See how your hand wants to explore the space around you and allow it to lead. Move just one hand or both. As you move, contemplate your call as artist and monk in the world. How do your hands serve as a vehicle for this calling?

3. When the song ends, rest for a moment and experience the music vibrating through you. Pay attention to your inner stirrings. Begin to notice if there is a shape or simple motion that feels like a satisfying conclusion to this experience. Create a gesture from this impulse and rest in that expression.

Reflection

4. When the experience feels complete, journal about what you noticed. Consider using colored pens or crayons to express in color what was moving in you. Do it without judgment. Simply notice the quality and journey of the experience.

5. As a conclusion, draw your attention back to the monastic commitments of obedience, stability, and conversion. Allow some time for reflection on them from this heart-centered and intuitive place of connection. Consider exploring in writing, color, or movement how these commitments support your work in the world as artist and monk. How do they encourage your ability to bless the world with what you do and who you are? Let this response arise from your embodied experience.

Poetry Writing Exploration

French Pantoum

Begin with free writing on the three commitments of obedience, stability, and conversion. Take about ten minutes to use each one as a prompt for written reflection and response.

When you think of obedience, what comes to mind? What colors, images, shapes, memories, and feelings are stirred in you? Use sensual, descriptive language as much as possible. Do this for stability and conversion as well.

What would it mean for you to take these commitments seriously as a part of your monastic and creative commitment? How do they support you in your ability to express your deepest self?

Write without judgment, allowing yourself to be surprised by what emerges in the process. Avoid editing as you go; now is the time to simply allow words to flow out and onto the page.

Once you are content with your level of reflection, reread your reflection and underline at least six phrases or images that stand out, that seem surprising, or that elicit an inner response of resonance or dissonance.

You'll use these phrases to create a pantoum. A *pantoum* is a form of poetry that uses the repetition of lines to create a poetic effect. Take the six underlined phrases from your writing and enter them into the French pantoum form that follows. Enter one of each of the six lines into lines one, two, three, four, six, and eight. Do this intuitively without focusing on the order. Once you have filled in the six phrases, go back and follow the instructions for the remaining lines on the form, and fill them in as directed.

Take a few minutes to read the poem that has emerged; you have now written a poem in the French pantoum form. Notice the feelings that arise as you read it. Feel free to edit a little bit for clarity or flow, but allow it to be a raw, immediate expression of your experience of and reflections on the monastic commitments, as well as their place in your life right now.

Sit with the poem and see what you discover; perhaps even do a lectio divina practice with a portion of it and see what happens.

French Pantoum

Stanza 1
Line 1:
Line 2:
Line 3:
Line 4:

Stanza 2
Line 5: (repeat of line 2 in stanza 1)
Line 6: (new line)
Line 7: (repeat of line 4 in stanza 1)
Line 8: (new line)

Stanza 3

Line 9: (repeat line 6 of stanza 2)
Line 10: (repeat line 3 of stanza 1)
Line 11: (repeat line 8 of stanza 2)
Line 12: (repeat line 1 of stanza 1)

Sitting in the morning sun I watch and listen
Not just with my eyes and ears but also with my heart and soul
Show me ancient ways of seeing
Teach me intuitive ways of listening
Not just with my eyes and ears but also with my heart and soul
I follow my path into this new way of living
Teach me intuitive ways of listening
To hear Spirit's whisperings in the wind
I follow my path into this new way of living
Show me ancient ways of seeing
To hear Spirit's whisperings in the wind
Sitting in the morning sun I watch and listen

—CATHY JOHNSON

HUMILITY: EMBRACING YOUR IMPERFECTIONS *and* LIMITATIONS

Humility — Telling the Truth about Our Earthiness

And the world cannot be discovered by a journey of miles, no matter how long, but only by a spiritual journey, a journey of one inch, very arduous and humbling and joyful, by which we arrive at the ground at our feet, and learn to be at home.

—WENDELL BERRY

As a Benedictine oblate, I have made a commitment to live out monastic values and practices in my everyday life. Perhaps one of the most profound values for me is humility, which is a virtue that does not elicit much awe or admiration in our culture. Humility seems outdated in our world of self-empowerment and self-esteem, and it negates much of the me-first values that our culture holds so dear.

Some reservations about humility are legitimate, especially for women. Abuse of humility can encourage passivity and low self-worth. An improper definition of humility can be used as a tool of oppression that imparts fear, guilt, or an abiding sense of failure. This is often an attempt to remind people of their proper "place" and to keep them from challenging institutions or those who hold power. False humility also exists when people deny how good they are as a means to elevate themselves.

There are different kinds of humility, and depending on the approach, humility could be life-giving or hostile. John Forman, a Benedictine oblate, writes:

> One key to differentiate life-giving humility from negating humility is the focus: Grace-given "humility" acknowledges both the individual self and the Self that transcends each of us, while hostile "humility" is entirely self-focused and, ultimately, consuming as it unevenly sees only the "created" and not the creator or that which sustains the created.

Hostile humility keeps us small and hinders full expression of our gifts.

The word *humility* is derived from *humus,* which means "earth." Humility is essentially about being rooted and grounded. Humility is also about truth and radical self-honesty in celebrating the unique gifts we have been given in service of others, while we recognize our limitations and woundedness.

In *Seeking God*, Esther De Waal writes that humility means to be "profoundly earthed" and to acknowledge the truth of our human condition. She suggests that if we want to know how humble we are, the first question to ask ourselves is: "How aware am I that anything I do in any way is part of the working out of God's will?" Humility demands that as a part of honesty, we also celebrate our blessings. We are taught to recognize our talents and skills as not of our own making. Rather, they are gifts we receive and hold in trust to give to our communities, and therefore, our gifts are not for ourselves alone. We are called to create not for our own satisfaction but to participate in the co-creation of a more just and beautiful world.

Remembering our earthiness and our human limitations is another important aspect of humility. As we will explore more in the chapter on simplicity, saying "no" is equally as important as saying "yes." Naming for ourselves where we are not being called is essential to discovering where we are being called to devote the fullness of our energy. We live in a world with so many good and worthy opportunities that we can feel pulled in many directions. Humility reminds us that we are not called to be all things to all people. Instead, we are to nurture our unique gifts and to recognize that self-care is good stewardship of those gifts.

Honoring our limits as creatures can be deeply liberating, as is surrendering our demanding inner perfectionism. How often do we resist beginning a creative project due to the fear that it will not live up to the image in our minds? Humility invites us to release those expectations and enter into the call of our gifts, knowing that it may look very differently from what we imagined.

Gently and compassionately recognizing our flaws can bind us closer to others and to God. We must have patience with the unfolding of our lives and the world, and understand that God's kingdom unfolds in God's time. When we do so, we discover that we are not solely responsible for saving the world. Acknowledging these limits can liberate us from our compulsions and frantic busyness and lead us toward recognizing our interdependence. In this way, each of our gifts contributes to the whole.

Humility is also about welcoming those experiences that create a sense of resistance in us. In his book on Benedictine humility, *A Guide to Living in the Truth,* Michael Casey reminds us that "a much more creative way of dealing with difficult texts is to take our negative reaction as an indication that there may be an issue beneath the surface with which we must deal." For instance, scripture passages that make us wrestle are often the ones that bear the greatest fruit, by revealing our own hidden places of resistance and fear. The same can be said of the creative process—the thing we most fear doing teaches us the most about our own hesitancies and angst. Humility invites us to embrace these challenges as doorways into deeper understanding of ourselves and God.

Tears of Compunction

Tears and weeping indicate a significant frontier in the way of the desert. They bespeak a promise. In fact, they are the only way into the heart.
—JOHN CHRYSSAVGIS

Humility is eliminating facades and embracing vulnerability—allowing ourselves to be seen without social convention, and presenting ourselves in all of our nakedness. Thomas Merton described this humility as the difference between the false self and true self. The fruit of humility is being comfortable with ourselves, our true selves, and being who God calls us to be because we have let go of living up to the expectations of others.

As creatures, we were made in the image of God, which imbues us with profound dignity. The reality of our nature, too, is that we each carry a brokenness that affects how we deal with others. To deny this truth is to perpetuate the suffering that comes as a result of our limitations. We each carry an array of inner voices that denounces our inherent goodness, demands an unattainable perfectionism, and lures us to fill our emptiness with compulsive behavior. Truthful living is the soul of humility. We are not divine; we are creatures. We are incomplete without God. We are not the source of our own being; we are broken and wounded.

Coming to this realization and setting aside all of the walls we have built up in our lives can be a challenging process. Deep sorrow wells up over what has been lost. We may find ourselves grieving for all the ways we have previously shut out intimacy and tenderness. We might discover a rawness and pain for previously preventing ourselves from living our creative longings until now. Tears might flow over the recognition of important truths about ourselves, truths that arise with an art experience.

Welcome the tears when they come. They will make room for the joy within you. Create space for the full spectrum, the whole ebb and flow of your own being. Give yourself permission to be in whatever season you find yourself, and trust that the resources and wisdom you need to continue the journey are here now in this moment.

The Ladder of Humility in the *Rule of St. Benedict*

We may call our body and soul sides of this ladder, into which our divine vocation has fitted the various steps of humility and discipline as we ascend.

—*Rule of St. Benedict*, 7:8

In chapter 7 of his *Rule,* St. Benedict presents us with the ladder of humility, inviting us on a journey that involves our whole self—body and soul together. The ladder is an ancient symbol of unity and integration, reaching from earth to heaven. St. Benedict reverses our expectations, however, and describes the process of descent as ascending, and ascent as descending. This is similar to the paradox of Jesus' life—of a community leader sitting down at table with those who were rejected, a master washing the feet of his disciples. These examples provide a vision of a new order and an image of encountering God in the most unexpected places. St. Benedict says that as we ascend into humility, so our capacity for love expands. In this way, letting go often brings us to new truth; surrendering our false expectations allows us to see more clearly. The practice of humility also leads us to a spirituality of radical newness and reversal— the kind that emerges from a life lived at the edges.

Notice this week when you are invited into a life-giving practice of humility: Where does recognizing and embracing your limitations free you to live more fully in the creative expression of your gifts? Where do you notice your own blocks and resistance to the practice of humility?

Contemplative Practices

Invitation

Sometimes when we approach art we think we have to go big to allow our expression to be grand and bold, to make a statement. But each of us has places in our inner world that are small and tender as well. This week consider the places in your life that could be freed by the grace of humility, of allowing imperfection, or of recognizing your need for rest and release. When does your need to have everything together block your creative expression?

Lectio Divina

In the Matthew's gospel, Jesus preaches a sermon on the mount about those who are blessed. This week's lectio divina invites you to enter into these Beatitudes with fresh eyes and ears. Imagine that each line is speaking to a part of you that has gone unattended. What are the places within you calling for more humility, more truthfulness, more earthiness?

> When he saw the crowds, he went up the mountain, and
> after he had sat down, his disciples came to him. He began
> to teach them, saying:

> *"Blessed are the poor in spirit, for theirs is the kingdom of heaven.*
> *Blessed are they who mourn, for they will be comforted.*
> *Blessed are the meek, for they will inherit the land.*
> *Blessed are they who hunger and thirst for righteousness, for they*
> *   will be satisfied.*
> *Blessed are the merciful, for they will be shown mercy.*
> *Blessed are the clean of heart, for they will see God.*
> *Blessed are the peacemakers, for they will be called children of*
> *   God.*
> *Blessed are they who are persecuted for the sake of righteousness,*
> *   for theirs is the kingdom of heaven.*
> *Blessed are you when they insult you and persecute you and utter*
> *   every kind of evil against you (falsely) because of me.*

> Rejoice and be glad, for your reward will be great in heaven.
> Thus they persecuted the prophets who were before you."

> —MATTHEW 5:1–12

Reflection Questions

- How might embracing your own imperfections be an act of grace and freedom? What are the limits you need to place on your energy so that you can live more fully into your gifts?
- Which of your "small selves," those tender and vulnerable places, need attention and blessing?

Guided Meditation

Blessing Our Small Selves

Sometimes we need to welcome our "small selves"—the poor, meek, humble parts of ourselves—to allow our big radiant selves to be in service to them. We need to welcome wrestling as a spiritual practice, rather than avoiding it. Perhaps there is something even more profound than all of the amazing things we are doing in the world. It is this simple unadorned self that is blessed. The smaller selves are blessed. Consider asking yourself: When I encounter moments when I am not in control, not putting my best foot forward, not creating the most "beautiful" art, can I relax into the moment? Can I accept the truth of my own imperfection?

This meditation is a contemplation of the Beatitudes while noticing which of our small selves wants voice today. You might engage only your imagination or use each section as a prompt for journal reflection.

Find a comfortable position, move your awareness into your body, and be present to the rhythm of your breathing for a few moments. Gently carry your awareness to the center of your heart, and make a physical connection for a moment by placing a hand on your heart.

Notice what you are feeling right now and allow yourself to have this experience. Continue breathing into this moment.

Remember that the mystics from across traditions tell us that God dwells in our hearts, the source of all compassion and love. Bring your awareness to this sacred presence within, and bring this infinite source of compassion to your experience. Imagine this presence as a "wise self" within you that can guide you.

Before Jesus began his public ministry, he went into the desert where the scriptures tell us he had angels ministering to him. Imagine yourself surrounded by a great cloud of witnesses who support you right now so that you are being held from within and without.

From this heart-centered place, I invite you to an interior journey through the Beatitudes. You will be resting into each one for a little while, making space to notice what stirs in you. The Beatitudes are not about our big radiant self, but about the tender, quiet self, or the self who has been shut out for some reason. Right now, in this safe place, you can invite the wisdom of your quiet self. Bring a beginner's mind, heart, and spirit to this experience, so you can open yourself to voices longing to speak.

Blessed are the poor in spirit, for theirs is the kingdom of heaven.

To be poor in spirit is to surrender yourself to something much bigger and vaster than your own ego. This poverty allows you to recognize your experience of exile in the world. God is present as the one who stirs in the depths of our hearts, not in the dominant ways we usually think out in the world. The experience of poverty and brokenness often acquaints us more deeply with the gift of simplicity as we discover what is most important. Where in your heart do you experience this call to simplicity, to finding that place where you and God meet? Notice what stirs in response, and be present to this experience.

Blessed are those who mourn, for they will be comforted.

Grief tells us that we loved deeply and that we are passionate. We are often unaware of the grief that we carry, that has been pushed aside in the rush of life or in the judgment that we should be done with its work. In reality, grief is slow. It rises and falls like a tide. Where in your heart do you experience a grief that lingers, that is calling for some attention? Notice the thoughts and feelings that respond, and be present to this experience.

Blessed are the meek, for they will inherit the earth.

To be meek means to have softened what is rigid within, to be like the fertile soil that receives its nourishment from the rain, allowing it to seep down into its substance. Is there a place within you that is longing to soften and yield? Is there a tender place longing to emerge and be expressed? What is the wisdom the earth has to offer you? Notice what stirs in response, and make some room to be present to this experience.

Blessed are the merciful, for they will receive mercy.

Those who are merciful are the ones who extend grace; they also receive grace in return. Where in your heart do you experience the longing for grace and mercy? Which part of you offers mercy and grace to others and which part resists? Notice what stirs in response, and make some room to be present to this experience.

Blessed are the pure in heart, for they shall see God.

To be pure in heart means to live in congruity between your inner life and your outer life; it means to live from an awareness of the Sacred Source who is pulsing in your own heart and in the world around you, moment by moment. Where in your life do you have a longing for integrity and for seeing God more clearly in each moment? Notice what stirs in response, and make some room to be present to this experience.

Blessed are the peacemakers, for they shall be called the children of God.

Your place of grief teaches you compassion and invites you to treat others with compassion. The peacemakers are those who seek to bring peace to their own hearts so that their interactions with others come from a place of peace. They are those who extend the practice of shalom into the world. Where in your heart do you experience the longing to make peace? What are you feeling in conflict with? Notice what stirs in response, and make room to be present to this experience.

Blessed are they who are persecuted for the sake of righteousness, for theirs is the kingdom of heaven. Blessed are you when they insult you and persecute you and utter every kind of evil against you (falsely) because of me.

What are the quiet voices within you that have been persecuted? How have you shut out the wisdom of these smaller selves? How might you begin to make more room for them to emerge?

As you complete your meditation, check in with yourself. Notice what you are feeling, and be compassionate with yourself. Connect again to your breath, rooting you in an awareness of God's presence each moment. As you gently begin to bring your awareness back to the room, remember the cloud of witnesses who stand beside you supporting you in this journey. See if any of them have faces you recognize.

Poetry Writing Exploration

Write Your Own Beatitudes

Following the meditation, allow some time for free writing, giving expression to your experience and what stirred within you. Consider writing some of your own beatitudes in response. What are the small, tender, and imperfect places you encountered? How might you offer them blessing through words? Consider beginning each line with "Blessed are the . . ." and paying attention to what comes to mind.

Visual Art Exploration

Photographing Wabi-Sabi— Wisdom from Buddhist Monastic Tradition

> *Wabi-sabi is a beauty of things imperfect, impermanent, and incomplete.*
> *It is a beauty of things modest and humble.*
> *It is a beauty of things unconventional.*
>
> —Leonard Koren
> *Wabi-Sabi for Artists, Designers,*
> *Poets and Philosophers*

The wisdom of Japanese Buddhism offers insights into the grace of humility for our lives as artists. The term *wabi-sabi* essentially refers to the beauty found in humility and imperfection and is based on certain truths observed in nature: all things are impermanent, all things are imperfect, and all things are incomplete. Everything in nature is in a state of becoming or dissolving. Wabi-sabi is rooted in the seasons and the sacred rhythms of the day and the year. In chapter 4, we explored the rise and fall, the emptiness and fullness, contained in each breath, day, month, year, and lifetime. Humility invites us to always remember that life is about both waxing and waning and to embrace the decline as much as we embrace the rise of things. It is to remember our earthiness.

Crispin Sartwell explores the meaning of *wabi-sabi* in his book, *Six Names of Beauty*, which is an exploration of aesthetic understanding in different cultures:

> Wabi as beauty is humility, asymmetry, and imperfection, a beauty of disintegration, of soil, of autumn leaves, grass in drought, crow feathers. For such reasons, an appreciation of wabi is an appreciation of the world and a certain sort of refusal of its transformation for delectation. Wabi as an aesthetic is a connection to the world in its imperfection, a way of seeing imperfection as itself embodying beauty . . . Sabi is a quality of stillness and solitude, a melancholy that is one of the basic human responses to and sources of beauty. . . . Thus wabi-sabi is an aesthetic of poverty and loneliness, imperfection and austerity, affirmation and melancholy. Wabi-sabi is the beauty of the withered, weathered, tarnished, scarred, intimate, coarse, earthly, evanescent, tentative, ephemeral.

Imagine what you consider beautiful and see if you can include death and decay. Autumn is the ultimate witness to the beauty found in death. Leaves explode with vibrant color just before their great release back to the earth.

For this week's art exploration, bring your camera with you on a walk. (A digital camera will be easiest, but a conventional one will also work.) Begin by closing your eyes for a few moments, centering yourself, and connecting to your breath. Consciously move your awareness from your head to your heart and breathe in the infinite source of compassion dwelling there. Then gently open your eyes, maintaining a soft gaze of receiving. Focus on your experience. As you move through the world, stay in this mode of receptivity and be present to the places of beauty in ugliness, decay, and death:

> Wabi-sabi is not found in nature at moments of bloom or lushness, but at moments of inception or subsiding. Wabi-sabi is not about gorgeous flowers, majestic trees, or bold landscapes. Wabi-sabi is about the minor and hidden, the tentative and ephemeral. . . . The beauty of wabi-sabi is, in one respect, the condition of coming to terms with what you consider ugly. (Leonard Koren, *Wabi-Sabi for Artists, Designers, Poets and Philosophers*)

Use your camera to receive images that come to you as you walk. Remain mentally present. When you return, review the images and reflect on what you discovered in this time of making space for the beauty of broken things. Notice if certain images resound with your own places of tenderness and vulnerability. Where have you been allowing this experience to hold you back from creative expression? How might these images serve as an invitation to release perfection and find beauty in imperfection?

> *Blessed are you who meets me where I am,*
> *in the quiet moments and hectic days.*
> *Blessed are you who comes like a whisper in my breath*
> *and spreads images of majesty before me.*
> *Blessed are you who comes incarnate through the smile*
> *of another, the touch of a hand or a kind word.*
> *Blessed are you who shines in the light of the candle*
> *and sings through the song of the sparrow.*
> *Blessed are you who meets me where I am—*
> *wretched, unholy, empty and longing to be filled.*
> *Blessed are you who greets me with a belly full*
> *of laughter under a starlit sky.*
> *Blessed are you who remains faithful through*
> *my questions and storms.*
> *Blessed are you who stands as sentinel in the night*
> *throughout my slumbering dreams or restless tossing.*
> *Blessed are you who I could name for an eternity*
> *and never be complete.*

Blessed are you who simply says, I AM,
and this is enough.
Amen. Amen. Amen.

—KAYCE STEVENS HUGHLETT

INNER HOSPITALITY *and* WELCOMING *the* STRANGER

Inner Hospitality

My own belief is that one regards oneself, if one is a serious writer, as an instrument for experiencing. Life — all of it — flows through this instrument and is distilled through it into works of art. How one lives as a private person is intimately bound into the work. And at some point, I believe one has to stop holding back for fear of alienating some imaginary reader or real relative or friend, and come out with personal truth. If we are to understand the human condition, and if we are to accept ourselves in all the complexity, self-doubt, extravagance of feeling, guilt, joy, the slow freeing of the self to its full capacity for action and creation, both as human being and artist, we have to know all we can about one another, and we have to be willing to go naked.

—MAY SARTON

In his *Rule*, St. Benedict wrote: "All guests who present themselves are to be welcomed as Christ, for he himself will say: 'I was a stranger and you welcomed me.'" The idea is that everyone who comes to the door of the monastery, and by extension the door to our lives, should be welcomed. This includes the poor, the traveler, the curious, those of a different religion, social class, or education. They are not welcomed merely as honored guests, but as windows onto the sacred presence. According to St. Benedict, our encounters with strangers—the unknown, the unexpected, foreign elements that spark our fear—are precisely the places where we are most likely to encounter God. This is a practice of outer hospitality.

Each of us has an inner monastery, or cave of the heart. Inner hospitality is to open our inner selves to everything we fear and reject in ourselves—our painful and dark feelings, our shadow side, our resistance, the secret things we do and desire. If we embrace St. Benedict's wisdom for our deepest selves, inner hospitality proceeds from the root of who we are. We learn to extend a welcome to the stranger who dwells inside of us.

We are each made up of multiple inner characters and voices. Some of them are invited to our inner table, while others are standing out in the rain, waiting to be let in to feast and to share their wisdom with us. In this book, we have been primarily focusing on the inner monk and artist; however, there are a host of selves and different energies within us. Rumi wrote a poem about the inner guesthouse that can accommodate the whole range of guests—the feelings we experience that we push back, resist, numb ourselves to—who might arrive at the inner door, and who might come bearing gifts for us.

Each of us contains a self—the true heart of who we are and the calm and non-anxious core we all possess—that is able to witness our internal process. It is often called the inner witness. This part of ourselves—described in different ways by many traditions as the spark of the soul, the virgin point, the sacred heart—can be fully present without anxiety and can offer radical hospitality to whomever or whatever knocks at our inner door.

In meditation, we cultivate our ability to be completely present to the rise and fall of our emotions. Rather than becoming detached or disassociated from them, we strive to fully experience our emotions without feeling carried away by their power. The art-making process offers the same invitation: to be present to what is happening within us by noticing the fears and judgments that come forth. The witness to this pattern in us is our compassion and curiosity—observing with love and tenderness. Witnessing is not about fixing something; witnessing is about entering into a relationship with what is and discovering the grace and gifts hidden there. We might then ask ourselves: Why is this feeling coming up right now in this time and place? What important message about God and me does this wave of feeling have to say to me? Where else in my life do I experience these voices?

Earlier in this book, I wrote about how the desert monks would say, "Go, sit in your cell, and your cell will teach you everything." The cell is both an internal and external place. We carry our monastic cell with us everywhere we go. "The reality of the cell should spill over into the reality of our life. The boundaries of our cell are gradually expanded to include every moment in our life and every detail in our world" (John Chryssavgis, *In the Heart of the Desert*). The cell is the place where we wrestle with our inner struggles and encounter God's presence in the midst of the wrestling.

In desert tradition, when we enter the cave of our heart, we encounter habits that developed from a core wound, often from childhood. These wounds distort the reality of who we are and lead us to compulsive acts. They need to be tended to and healed, which is challenging because they connect us to our deepest vulnerability. One strand of desert tradition views passion negatively, as something to be eradicated from the soul. Reading these early monks, we sometimes encounter the language of battling with the passions. However, the dominant teaching for the desert mothers and fathers was that passions are positive; passions are natural and neutral impulses originated in God but distorted and misdirected in our human efforts to suppress them. Language is more positive, such as "knowing the passions," where knowing means loving and embracing. "The aim is to illumine them, not eliminate them; they are not to be destroyed but mastered and even transfigured" (John Chryssavgis, *In the Heart of the Desert*).

Abba Isaiah, one of the desert fathers, claims that all passions, including those that result in anger, jealousy, and lust, are given to us by God for a particular and sacred purpose. Coming to know these passions, how they were formed and what they desire, is a healing experience. We begin to reclaim all the parts of ourselves—what we might consider "good" or "bad"—and in the process we become more whole by accepting the fullness of who we are.

> If God is right there in the midst of our struggle, then our aim is to stay there. We are to remain in the cell, to stay on the road, not to forego the journey or forget the *darkness*. It is all too easy for us to overlook the importance of struggle, preferring instead to secure peace and rest, or presuming to reach the stage of love prematurely. It is always easier to allow things to pass by, to go on without examination and effort. Yet, struggling means living. It is a way of fully living life and not merely observing it. It takes much time and a great effort to unite the disparate, disjointed, and divided parts of the self into an integrated whole. During this time and in this effort, the virtue of struggle was one of the non-negotiables in the spiritual way of the desert. The Desert Fathers and Mothers speak to us with authority, because they are in fact our fellow travelers. They never claim to have arrived, they never indicate having completed the journey. (John Chryssavgis, *In the Heart of the Desert*)

John Chryssavgis is speaking of the monastic commitment to conversion—the recognition that we are continuously growing and that this process is never completed. The temptation of the spiritual life is to avoid pain, to believe that being "spiritual" means always being full of peace and grace, when in fact the whole teaching of the desert tradition focuses on the need to stay fully present to the often challenging and painful dynamics that happen within us. This is an area where stability roots us, reminding us not to run away from feelings we dislike. In obedience, we are called to listen to these disowned parts of ourselves and respond to what they are asking of us.

How do you welcome the range of your feelings without being swept away by them? One way is to cultivate your inner witness and connect regularly with your calm, non-anxious, compassionate, core self. Meditation can nurture our ability to sit and observe the fluctuations of our inner lives without resisting or seizing any particular moment. When we offer ourselves the space to simply be with whatever is happening inside, without judgment, we begin to see that each of those feelings passes with time. Through art and journaling we can engage in an active dialogue with those parts of ourselves we find threatening or depleting.

This week, when you notice yourself resisting an inner voice or shutting your inner door on it, take some time to intentionally invite this voice inside to the table. Ask it what it has come to tell you. Listen past the first layer, which may sound ugly or painful, and tend to the layers underneath. This takes time, much like growing in intimacy with a friend. Our rejected selves will need some coaxing.

When we receive guests as windows into the sacred presence, we are choosing to live and relate from a more intentional and reverential place. We have practiced being present to the sacred in each hour and with each object around us, and now we bring that attention even more consciously within. When we engage in a dynamic encounter with what we fear, it releases its power on us, and new wisdom and energy are released. It is in this place of hospitality to the unknown where we encounter God.

The poet Naomi Shihab Nye writes: "Before you know kindness as the deepest thing inside, / you must know sorrow as the other deepest thing." We learn to make space within ourselves because on the other side of the voices that disturb us we find the gift of wisdom waiting for us. When we learn this landscape of sorrow, we can also enter into solidarity with others who are sorrowful. Then both our art making and living will come from a deeper and more authentic place. Our capacity for sorrow and joy are in proportion to one another.

Contemplative Practices

Invitation

This week's focus is about getting in touch with our deepest vulnerabilities and welcoming them, rather than pushing them away as we might be conditioned to do. Be gentle with yourself in this process. As you read the lesson and contemplate the meditation, give yourself permission to be wherever you need to be. Make no mistake, this is very hard work, and yet I believe it is some of the most valuable work we can do. This is the heart of the monastic path, of being present to the sacredness of everything — including ourselves.

This is an invitation to be tender with your delicate places and to notice your resistance. For a few minutes, simply breathe and create some room inside for those neglected or forgotten parts of yourself. Inevitably, grief will arise from all of the fighting you have done. Simply notice this as well, welcoming it as part of the journey toward wholeness and the joy found in authentic, creative living.

Lectio Divina

This week's text comes from the letter to the Hebrews. It is about what happens when we welcome those for whom we normally feel fear or resistance. Allow yourself to savor the words in prayer and listen for God's invitation rising up from your encounter.

> *Do not neglect*
> *to show hospitality*
> *to strangers.*
> *For by this some have entertained*
> *angels without knowing it.*
>
> —HEBREWS 13:2

Reflection Questions

- How do you welcome life (be it in the form of experience, feelings, thoughts, nature/creation, or people)?
- What are the inner voices with which you experience the most resistance?
- How does the work of inner hospitality nourish both your inner monk and your inner artist?
- How does claiming yourself as a monk and an artist require you to draw on the full spectrum of your humanity?
- Where are the places in your life and art where your hidden voices get expressed?

Guided Meditation

Welcoming Our Inner Selves at the Door

This week's lesson introduces probably one of the most challenging and most rewarding of the monastic-based practices. In this guided meditation, you will be invited into an experience of inner hospitality. I will suggest to you a simple structure for beginning to make space for the feelings and voices you might usually resist. You don't always have to enter into the dialogue part of the meditation. The initial part of the practice of simply making room for our emotions can be powerful, especially as over time we develop the habit of not shutting ourselves down.

Take a few moments now to begin to connect with yourself. Notice how your body is feeling in this moment and shift to find a comfortable position. See if you feel safe from intrusions on your time right now, as it is important to be able to move into this experience without distraction.

Begin to pay attention to your breath, noticing the natural rhythm of inhaling and exhaling without trying to change anything. Just be present to this life-giving rhythm that sustains you moment by moment even when you are unconscious of it.

Allow your breath to gently carry your awareness from your head (your thinking, analyzing, and judging center) down to your heart—that place of intuitive and feeling presence.

Place your hand on your heart and experience a physical connection to your inner monastery, to the place that mystics from across time and traditions have told us is the place God dwells. Take a few moments to become fully present to your heart as a dwelling place for the Divine Presence. Experience the expansiveness of this space and breathe into it.

Become aware of this place in yourself, the spark of the soul, which is your inner witness. Remember that your inner witness is the non-anxious, calm, compassionate, and curious presence you can bring to all of your life experiences. This is your core self, which is able to welcome life's struggles and offer you a resting place, an anchor in the midst of your inner wrestling.

Begin to notice your feelings. See if you can welcome them without trying to change anything. Simply experience your emotions in their fullness, being present without judgment. If you harbor grief, open yourself to the sadness; if you sense anger, let it reside in you; if you feel anxious, make room for this experience. Allow whatever is true for you right now to be. Experience your feelings without acting on them.

Become conscious of your inner witness again and bring compassion to this moment. Let yourself be gently aware of all that is moving in you without dissociating or disconnecting, and without letting yourself be carried away on the tide of your feelings.

As you continue to create space within you for your feelings, notice if you have any physical sensations rising. Just be present to what your body is experiencing. See if there is a place in your body where this feeling resides and simply acknowledge it.

When thoughts rise up in judgment, allow the compassionate and curious part of yourself to make more room for your feelings. Continue to breathe, knowing that you are being supported in this moment.

Begin to focus on one emotion right now. Recognize which one wants your attention and make some space within you to receive it more deeply. As you connect with this emotion, imagine that it has a voice with which to speak to you. Try not to think this through; merely receive whatever comes. Staying present to the emotional experience, welcome it in and ask if there is something this voice wants to tell you. Ask where this voice originates and why it first developed. Ask what it wants from you now and see if you can receive a response. If you'd like, you can pause in this meditation and spend a few minutes being present to how it wants to speak to you, continuing to make room for your feeling experience. Resume when you come to a place where the reflection feels complete for now.

Once you have moved through this dialogue, thank this inner voice for its wisdom. Connect again with your breath and allow its rhythm to slowly and gently carry you back to the room. Take some time to journal or draw what you experienced. You might follow with the art exploration outlined next.

Whenever you experience a difficult or painful emotion, take a moment to pause and simply receive it. Observe any discomfort associated with the feeling, and make room for it within you. In that moment, connect to your breath and your heart center, and imagine breathing it in to that wide space within you.

Visual Art Exploration

Drawing Your Inner Selves

Materials needed: paper and oil pastels or crayons.

"Gush art" is a term coined by Jane Comerford, my colleague in the expressive arts. Essentially, gush art is about quieting ourselves and listening deeply to what is stirring within and then giving it form through color and shape, solely to express our inner movements. Gush art is not meant to be beautiful or hung in a gallery. It is a wonderful practice when your inner critics start to rise up. Give yourself permission to make "bad" art. By "bad," I simply mean art that is purely for self-exploration, for discovering the images moving within, and for honoring the beauty found in truthfulness—art in which you can let go of striving for some particular outcome.

For this process, allow yourself between thirty minutes and an hour. You might begin by using the previous meditation or by spending a few moments connecting to your breath and receiving the gift of the breath of life in each moment by exhaling, releasing, and surrendering any judgments or criticism. Don't force this process; simply allow the breath to give you a physical experience of being filled with life and then give an embodied release.

Gently bring your awareness from your head down to your heart center. Place your hand on your heart to make a physical connection. Savor this life-giving rhythm of breath and heartbeat, which sustains you moment by moment. Let your pulse and the rise and fall of your breathing remind you of your earthiness. Take a moment to experience whatever you may be feeling right now, providing space for your emotions without trying to change them. Then remember what the mystics tell us—that the infinite source of compassion dwells here within us. Breathe in that compassion, allowing it to fill any tender places.

From this heart-centered space, spread some paper out in front of you and see if there is an inner voice that wants attention today, one that you have resisted in the past. Perhaps it is the voice of perfectionism or judgment. Stay connected to the wisdom of your inner witness as you welcome in this part of yourself, cultivating an openness to hear what it has to say through image. Pay attention to the colors you feel drawn to.

You might want to play some quiet music, or you can let the silence hold you. Allow about fifteen to twenty minutes to explore through color and shape what is moving through you. Give form to the texture and quality of this voice, simply honoring its presence. Be present to your inner process and notice the thoughts that rise up. If judgment or analysis starts to settle in, gently return to your breath and your heart. Remember that the purpose of this time is exploration, and you have full permission to make "bad" art. You might even want to explore what that would mean for you, letting yourself enter into the experience with the intention of having it look as childlike or raw as possible.

When you feel like you have done enough, close your eyes for a moment. Connect again to your heart and then gaze with love and compassion on what has emerged in this experience. Observe without judging. Take time to journal about the process and what you are beginning to discover.

You can repeat this exercise for each emotion. Allowing these emotions to have a presence on the page can help diffuse their power. If we welcome in and listen to the voices of our emotions, we may discover that they are trying to protect us from something that is really no longer a threat. When we release our resistance, we may find wisdom. The voice that has hindered us for so long becomes an ally in our transformation.

If you ever find yourself engaging in an inner dialogue when making a decision, and you say, "there's a part of me that wants to . . ." or "there's a part of me that won't let me . . ." try engaging in this art exercise. Give form to these thoughts and permit them voices and space in a calm, non-anxious environment.

Writing Exploration

Fairy Tale

Write a fairy tale about some of the inner voices and characters you tend to resist or block out. Begin with "once upon a time" and create a story about a mythical gathering where your inner voices are invited into your inner monastery to sit down together. Tell the fairy tale in past tense. Give each inner voice a name and capitalize the name. You might consider exaggerating or embellishing the setting of the gathering, emphasizing the colors and the surroundings. Notice the details of the place where your story wants to unfold. Give descriptions of each character's appearance, tone of voice, and way of interacting, bringing each one to life. Add the words "always" and "never" wherever you can, and use as many details as possible. The story doesn't have to end "happily ever after." Read your fairy tale aloud. See what insights or new connections appear from this form. Most of all, have fun with it.

Of Caves and Hidden Things: A Fairy Tale

Once upon a time there was a secret cave on the edge of a mountain, deep inside a forest. The entrance was small and easily overlooked, tucked darkly between the mossy roots of an ancient oak. But the inside of the cave was huge, with vaulted ceilings like an underground cathedral.

In the middle of the cave stood an old round wooden table, with rough-hewn oak chairs around it, except for one chair, which was made of stone, for reasons I'll explain in a minute.

Occasionally, and usually when the moon was full, an ill-assorted group would gather in this secret place and take their places around the table.

There was the green-eyed Witch: tall, thin and beautiful in her austerity, powerful and self-contained. There was the Adventuress, curvy yet muscular, with her penchant for dressing in various dashing ensembles. And there was the Ore Golem, a shapeless iron mountain of a man-creature, with lava oozing from the cracks in his skin. It was for the Ore Golem that the stone chair was kept, because the furnace of heat from beneath his crusted iron flanks had already made short work of several wooden chairs.

Actually, there was a fourth member of the group, but she had a tendency to keep to the background, and because the other three took her so much for granted they sometimes forgot she was there. Her name was Mother. She was short and plump, with dimpled cheeks, strong practical hands and wise, calm eyes. She always smelled of baking bread.

One night, the four of them gathered around the table to discuss what was going on in the forest.

They were disturbed by how narrow-minded the forest people were becoming. Back when the forest was new, the four around the wooden table had been part of its life, but as the years went by they became increasingly feared and marginalized, and had begun to stay hidden, out of sight. Lately they had begun to sense the beginnings of active persecution. Small knots of forest folk were gathering in the ale houses, their heads close together, murmuring about the power and gravity of the Witch, the unseemly freedom of the Adventuress and her frolicking, rollicking life, and the unstoppable fiery anger of the Ore Golem. (They, too, had a tendency to forget about Mother.)

"It's only a matter of time before they come for us, before they hunt us down," said the Adventuress (who today was dressed as a pirate queen). "I love a good fight, you know that, and there's a new blunderbuss I'm longing to try out, but there are too many of them, they'll kill us all. We must leave this place now, set sail for a younger country."

The Witch looked down her elegant nose (shuddering slightly as she remembered the khaki Edwardian bloomers and lace-up bodice the Adventuress had worn for their last gathering). "It's not death we should fear," she said. "They don't want us dead, they want us like them. They want to suck the energy and individuality from us so we don't threaten them, don't show them what they could become if they only had the courage. I should conjure great magic to calm the people, to make them sleep, so we can have the forest to ourselves."

"Aaarrhh gahrr rooarrh," said the Ore Golem as he thumped the table, leaving a large fist-shaped scorch mark. His speech was difficult for an outsider to understand, although the fact that he was always angry and the sheer power of his rage were pretty unmistakable. The others, who had known him from a little cinder and understood his speech, knew he was declaring that the forest folk had better not come anywhere near him if they knew what was good for them, or he would burn the forest to the ground and them all in it.

So round and round they went, discussing late into the night what they should do. Their voices rose and fell as they argued their own position, and the face of the full moon moved across the sky in a perfect arc. (She had her own ideas about all this, but what they were this story doesn't tell us.)

Finally, as the stars were beginning to fade, Mother cleared her throat. The others were startled because as usual they'd forgotten she was there, and they turned to face her.

"So as I understand it," she said in her quiet voice, "you are talking about three possibilities: running away and taking our gifts with us; using stealth to deny the forest folk their awareness and free will; or utterly destroying the people and the ground they stand on."

"I want to suggest a fourth possibility. I don't know if it will work. We walk out together now into the forest daylight. We greet the forest people with love and we show them that inside each of them there is power, magic, courage, adventure, fun, and fierce pure anger. That these things are part of what it means to be fully human, fully whole."

Mother raised her hands to quell the clamor threatening to break out around the table. "And there's only one way to show them this. It is to use my own gift, which you'd all do well to remember more often: the limitless power of compassion."

The others fell silent as Mother stood, pulling herself up to her not very great height. "So, what do you want to do?"

— Tess Giles Marshall

CREATIVE COMMUNITY

Finding Your Spiritual Community

To be a monk today or someone seeking to incorporate monastic values into his or her own life presumes being a part of a community of friends, people with whom a person can share the counsels of the heart and speak a language of the heart to one another.

—EDWARD C. SELLNER

Many of us have multiple communities. I consider my primary community to be my marriage. This is the place of my most intimate encounters with another person. My husband supports me wholeheartedly, though we also wrestle with one another, occasionally bumping up against each other's edges with conflicting desires and needs. My dog Winter is also a part of this core community, offering her faithful presence and witness to me each day. I have a few very close friends with whom I can share my deepest struggles, who hold me lovingly in that space and witness my own unfolding. These are women who support me in the realization of my dreams and with whom I also sometimes struggle when we misunderstand one another. I meet regularly with a spiritual director as well. This wise, older man has taught me much about being present to my dream life, my inner doubts and struggles, and the wisdom of my ancestors.

My Benedictine oblate community is my primary spiritual community, where I experience the true meaning of church. For me, this means having a group of fellow pilgrims who are also seeking ways through ancient practices to live a meaningful life in a complex world. This community does not offer easy answers, but is willing to walk alongside me in my doubts and questions.

I also experience a great cloud of witnesses, especially my blood ancestors, as a community of support in my life. I often find myself calling upon my deceased grandmothers, both of whom had to give up work they loved (one as a dancer, and the other as a teacher) when they got married. I knew only one grandmother, but I carry both of their longings in me. I live out my life in their honor and ask them to lift me up. I call upon the communion of saints, including St. Benedict, his sister St. Scholastica, St. Hildegard of Bingen, and others who have lived the monastic life with deep integrity and wisdom.

Beyond these core layers, I am connected to people because of something we share. With my neighbors, I share a love for the vibrant, urban place in which we live, and I commune with fellow spiritual directors for mutual support and ongoing spiritual growth. I am connected to many other circles that gather around shared values and, of course, to the wider communities of city, country, globe, and creation.

I invite you to reflect on the core members of your circle. Sometimes we need to seek a spiritual community, but sometimes we need to simply recognize the layers of support that already exist in our lives and allow them to become a more intentional element. Who are the people who celebrate your gifts with you? Who do you naturally turn to for support when you feel a new call rising up within you? Who are the people in your life with whom you speak a "language of the heart"? Who supports your creative longings wholeheartedly?

Love can be demanding. Making our relationships a priority and serving even when we don't feel like it are not always easy. Love necessitates that we allow the people in our lives to be themselves without our wishing they were different. In our challenges with others, we are invited to welcome dissonance and notice the stirrings in our own hearts.

In chapter 3 of Benedict's *Rule*, he writes that when any important decision is to be made in the monastery, the whole community is gathered because "the Lord often reveals what is better to the younger" (*Rule of St. Benedict,* 3:3). Sometimes our vision is clouded by our own expectations. St. Benedict invites us to welcome in the wisdom of everyone in our community. Often others can see aspects of ourselves that we cannot. Consider asking someone you trust deeply to tell you how they see your gifts at work in the world and the places where you seem to hold yourself back. Receive these words with reverence and humility, and welcome in what they might have to teach you about your own creative journey.

It's likely that many of you have experienced the pain of being in community, the hurt from rejection or devaluation, of not being welcomed home. Exile is a powerful archetypal experience in the human journey. The story of the Exodus ripples across time as one example of the longing for a distant home. Being the one who dwells on the borders and serves as a visionary for the community is challenging when your vision is beyond what the others can see. This becomes evident in the responsibility of calling others to conversion. Challenging people to change can be uncomfortable and threatening, so the one who is offering the new vision is often thwarted.

Soul Friend

The friend who can be silent with us in a moment of despair or confusion, who can stay with us in an hour of grief and bereavement, who can tolerate not knowing . . . not healing, not curing . . . that is a friend who cares.

—HENRI J.M. NOUWEN

In the desert, Celtic, and Benedictine traditions, it was considered essential to have some kind of soul-level relationship with another person who was further along the path of conscious awareness and spiritual practice. Many of you are probably familiar with the Gaelic term *anam cara,* which means "soul friend."

In the fourth and fifth centuries, St. Cassian went to the Egyptian desert to learn about the importance of a relationship with a spiritual elder— "a wise, holy, and experienced person who can act as a teacher and guide for an individual or community." Of the many graces of their spiritual lives, an experienced guide was the greatest gift, according to the desert monks. *Abba* was the term for a male wisdom-bearer and *amma* for a female wisdom-bearer. These elders were also referred to as *pneumatikos mater* or *pater*: "a spirit-bearer who acts as a kind of foster parent or midwife of souls" (Edward C. Sellner, *Finding the Monk Within*). St. Cassian firmly believed that God's guidance and wisdom comes most often through human mediation and the encounter with the desert elders. Age does not guarantee this kind of wisdom, which comes through a person who also has been formed in apprenticeship to another wise one.

Joan Chittister, in *Wisdom Distilled from the Daily,* describes the four main elements of Benedictine spirituality as "the Scriptures, the text of the Rule, wise leaders, and the insight, life experience, and circumstances of the community or family in which we live." The focus of monastic life is a communal act. We are dependent on the wisdom of others and we must consider the whole community—including the community of creation—in discerning our daily actions. The *Rule* begins with the words "listen with the ear of your heart." Monastic practice is very much about listening to the truth of the sacred presence in a given moment. Seeking out wise elders and mentors in our lives is an essential element of cultivating this capacity to listen. Consider the people in your life who live with creative vitality and contemplative presence. Seek out mentors who have embraced their inner monks and inner artists. Speak with them about the ways in which they sustain themselves and nurture their way of being in the world.

Witnessing in Community

Striving for a common goal, with shared philosophy and values, can make the difficulties of

*living with others easier. Yet one definition of
true community is that it includes individuals
who are difficult or even abhorrent. And here is
our true challenge as mystics in the world: to
create community with those who are so different from us that we feel we have nothing in common with them. As our world becomes smaller,
through a growing common culture, the true test
of community will be our tolerance for our most
profound differences and love for the most challenging among us.*

—WAYNE TEASDALE

Just as we are called to cultivate our internal witness through the
practice of inner hospitality, we are called to be a witness to each other
through outer hospitality—to be fully present to the sorrow and despair
of another without rushing to console in order to circumvent our own
discomfort. Providing the opportunity for others to experience the full
spectrum of what is stirring within them is a rare gift beyond measure.
When we do this actively for ourselves, we nurture our capacity to offer
this gift to another person. If we continue to run away from our own grief,
anger, resistance, or even joy, then we will not be able to stay present
when a friend needs us. The inner work we do, we also do on behalf of
our community.

Because I treasure friends and other supportive people in my life, I
am able to walk into the feelings of despair when they come. Because
I regularly nurture the ability of my inner witness to be present to the
guests arriving at my inner door, I am able to welcome them in. When
the difficult feelings arrive, I breathe deeply and make space to listen to
their messages, rather than resisting them and leaving them banging on
the door. Some days this is easier than others, but most of the time it is
hard work. As Rumi said so wisely on welcoming each emotion into the
internal guesthouse: I will treat each guest honorably, as a guide much
wiser than myself.

In that act of hospitality, I will walk in solidarity with those who
are shrouded in pain. I will gradually understand the necessity of kindness, and I will discover moments of wonder. Several years ago, while I

was working with another wise spiritual director, I experienced the pain of rejection with no explanation. The director invited me to walk in the landscape of that rejection, to know its contours intimately, to confront its pain. In this way, I would also be able to walk alongside others who suffer from that same pain, knowing the interior of that experience.

Owning, acknowledging, and revealing the truth of one's experience and having this truth witnessed by another with reverence and care are essential in the journey toward wholeness. Witnessing means listening rather than analyzing or interpreting. Our compassionate embrace of another's difficult voice assists him or her in the process of integration. Having someone in our own lives—a spiritual director, a soul friend, a wise companion—who can offer this gift, is invaluable.

Communion of Saints

"All the company of heaven" means everybody
we ever loved and lost, including the ones we
didn't know we loved until we lost them or didn't
love at all. It means people we never heard of.
It means everybody who ever did—or at some
unimaginable time in the future ever will—come
together at something like this table in search of
something like what is offered at it.

—FREDERICK BUECHNER

In the Christian tradition, we do not limit our community of support to those who live at the same time as we do. We invoke "so great a cloud of witnesses surrounding us" (Heb 12:1) to support us and offer us wisdom for the journey as those who have traveled this path already.

In his quotation above, Buechner is referring to the gathering of the community at the altar table, which includes "all the company of heaven." If we find altars throughout the world, as Benedict's *Rule* invites us to consider, we might remember the whole communion of saints who have also come to the art table searching for ways to give meaningful expression to their hopes and longings, whether through paint or words, baking bread or planting seeds in the fertile soil.

In the introduction to this book, I mentioned Hildegard of Bingen as a patron saint of my journey toward becoming a Benedictine oblate, since it was through her that I found myself called to this monastic path. Her witness as both monk and artist showed me this ancient way of being in the world. As monks and artists, we might consider calling upon a great witness to the living of this way of life.

Consider a saint or poet from the Christian tradition or another who exemplifies the integration of contemplative practice and creative expression. Learn more about this person's life and writings. See what wisdom you glean from entering more deeply into this person's world. As you begin prayer or your own creative work, consider calling on this person for support. Ask him or her to be present to you in this time and to help you to listen to what wants to emerge in the process. There might be an artist from your own life who was an inspiring figure. Consider ancestors from your own family who can offer valuable support, wisdom, and ongoing insight.

Contemplative Practices

Invitation

Consider the ways you might welcome more support in your life and honor those places where you already have sacred companions who help you navigate life's terrain. How might you expand this circle and welcome in other monks and artists with whom to journey?

Lectio Divina

Lynn Ungar is one of my favorite poets because of her lush use of language to evoke the wisdom of the natural world for our everyday lives. Enter into prayer this week with her poem "Flower Communion" and listen for what invitation emerges.

What a gathering—the purple
tongues of iris licking out
at spikes of lupine, the orange
crepe skirts of poppies lifting
buttercup and daisy.
Who can be grim
in the face of such abundance?
There is nothing to compare,
no need for beauty to compete.
The voluptuous rhododendron
and the plain grass
are equally filled with themselves,
equally declare the miracles
of color and form.
This is what community looks like
this vibrant jostle, stem by stem
declaring the marvelous joining.
This is the face of communion,
the incarnation once more
gracefully resurrected from winter.
Hold these things together
in your sight—purple, crimson,
magenta, blue. You will
be feasting on this long after
the flowers are gone.

—Lynn Ungar

Reflection Questions

- Where in your life do you experience community on a soul level? Who are your soul friends and mentors? Are there ancestors upon whom you might call for support?
- What is your definition of true community? Which members of your community do you find challenging? How might they be at the heart of your spiritual practice? What is the invitation of hospitality in your own soul tribe or sacred flock?
- Do you have a friend with whom you can rest in your despair or confusion and who doesn't try to move you toward happiness? Are you able to be this presence to others?

Guided Meditation

Circles of Community

To begin the meditation, find a comfortable position sitting or lying down. Become aware of your body. Notice how your body feels, simply being present to physical sensations, welcoming the body's delight and discomfort.

Connect to your breath, deepening it gently. As you inhale, imagine God breathing life into you. As you exhale, allow yourself to experience a moment of release and surrender to this moment, becoming fully present. Take a couple of cycles of breath to simply notice this life-sustaining rhythm that continues even when you are unaware of it.

In your imagination, gently allow your breath to carry your awareness from your head (which is your thinking, analyzing, judging center) down to your heart (where you experience life from a place of greater integration, feeling, and intuition). Consider placing your hand on your heart to experience a physical connection with your heart center and draw your awareness to this place. Take a moment to notice what you are feeling, allowing whatever is the truth of your experience without judging it or trying to change it. Then breathe in the infinite compassion of God who dwells in your heart, and allow it to fill you and all of your feelings. Rest for a moment in that experience of the fullness of compassion. Hold for a moment the image of the cave of your heart and savor this presence within you, this place of simplicity and silence.

Breathing in and out again, widen your inner gaze to include your family members, close friends, companion animals, and members of your spiritual community. Breathe in that infinite source of compassion, and exhale allowing it to fill each of them. Savor this experience and notice whatever stirs in you in response.

Breathing in and out again, begin to contemplate the neighborhood in which you live. How does your community support you in small and large ways? Who are the people who work at the grocery store or the gas station whose presence facilitates your ability to thrive here? What are the places of refuge and sanctuary nearby? Is there a park or a beach you go to for solace?

Continue to be aware of your breath and allow your inner gaze to widen and encompass the global community. Imagine cultures and traditions across the earth present at this very same moment, each trying to discover meaningful ways to live. Savor this awareness, recognizing that you are a part of this thriving diversity.

Return to your breath and meditate on the whole matrix of creation, all living creatures, plants, and animals. Teilhard de Chardin described his vision of creation as the "breathing together of all things." Take a moment to inhale and exhale and imagine the life-giving exchange of oxygen and carbon dioxide with plant life that sustains you. Then imagine the rhythmic breath of living organisms across the planet. Recognize your life as a part of this vast community of nature.

Then shift your perspective slightly from spatial boundaries to temporal ones. In your inner gaze, become aware of your ancestors, the communion of saints, or your cloud of witnesses who have walked this earth before you. See how your roots extend back through history, connecting you to hundreds and thousands of stories through times of celebration and grief. Take a few moments to honor the community of people whose lives have led to your existence in this moment of time.

Allow your heart to open wide in gratitude for how these people, creatures, and landscapes, across time and space, have shaped who you are now. Embrace the fullness of your place in this community. Pause to make space for how you feel; pay attention to images, emotions, and memories.

Connecting to your breath, slowly narrow your gaze back again, while holding an awareness of the vast expanse in which you are embedded. With the eyes of your heart, honor your ancestors, the matrix of creation, the global community, the place where you live, your landscape, and the circle of friends and family who support you. Feel that expansiveness within your body.

Bring your focus back to your own heart. With your inner gaze, take in this moment. Notice what you are experiencing right now after taking this interior journey. See yourself as supported across space and time.

Connect gently to your breath again and allow its rhythm to slowly bring you back to the room. Allow a few moments to journal any insights or awareness that feels significant.

Movement Exploration

Walking the Spiral

The spiral is an ancient symbol of integration and non-linear experi-ence. In the spiral, we bring together both sides of the brain and discover that all of our life is present to us as a rich resource for the present moment. Walking the spiral slowly and with intention can be a very potent activity.

It is quite simple to create an indoor spiral out of a long piece of yarn laid out on the floor. You need a room with a fairly large open space in the middle, so maybe a living room where the furniture can be pushed back against the wall, or a church or community space if you can borrow a room for an hour or so. If the space is accessible, you could create a spiral outside on the grass, using stones and leaves.

Use several yards of yarn to form a spiral on the floor with a path wide enough to walk. Begin laying it out from the center and create up to four loops—even if you only have two loops around, they are enough for this practice. I recommend laying out the yarn clockwise so that the path you walk is counterclockwise, and place a lighted candle in the center.

You might begin your walk of the spiral with a question. Consider holding one question gently in your heart, perhaps about the role of com-munity in supporting your inner monk and artist. Release your thinking about the question, simply letting it go and resting into silence.

Prepare to enter the spiral in the same way you might walk a laby-rinth. Take some time to center yourself, focusing on this journey, and invite the presence of your community across time and space to be with you. Ask that they be present to you with each step, supporting you and encouraging you. Listen for the invitation in each moment, keeping an open mind and heart, free of expectation.

Take as long as you need to reach the center, listening for the wisdom and guidance of the cloud of witnesses as you travel.

Pause at the center to receive whatever gift is offered there and rest in the still point.

Walk intentionally back out, carrying the gifts received back out into the world. As you reach the last step, pause again to offer gratitude for the ways the ancestors and those in your community have been with you during this time. Take some time following the walk to sit in stillness and then write, draw, or paint what you experienced, noticing if there is a new invitation or response to the question with which you began.

> *She extends the invitation: Find Your Way as a Monk, Your Path as*
> *an Artist.*
> *We come from east and west, from north and south,*
> *A virtual community gathering at Table to receive and give, to rest*
> *and to be.*
> *With collages, altars, and haikus, fairy tales, photos and rules,*
> *voices are heard, gifts are claimed, and our souls find*
> *wholeness.*
> *We come from east and west, from north and south,*
> *Opening wells of creativity and inner rhythms of the sacred.*
> *With collages, altars, and haikus, fairy tales, photos and rules,*
> *voices are heard, gifts are claimed, and our souls find*
> *wholeness.*
> *By the workings of Spirit we commit to create and listen, to risk*
> *and offer healing.*
> *Opening wells of creativity and inner rhythms of the sacred,*
> *A virtual community gathering at Table to receive and give, to rest*
> *and to be.*
> *By the workings of Spirit we commit to create and listen, to risk*
> *and offer healing.*
> *She extends the invitation: Find Your Way as a Monk, Your Path as*
> *an Artist.*
>
> —CATHY JOHNSON

NATURE *as* SOURCE *of* REVELATION *and* INSPIRATION

Kinship with Creation

How necessary it is for monks to work in the fields, in the rain, in the sun, in the mud, in the clay, in the wind: these are our spiritual directors and our novice-masters. They form our contemplation. They instill us with virtue. They make us as stable as the land we live in.

—THOMAS MERTON

The natural world has formed Christian awareness and practice since ancient times. There is a wonderful story about St. Kevin, who was spending the season of lent in a small hut in the desert. At one point as he lifted his hand through the window to heaven, a blackbird landed on his palm, and laid her egg there. St. Kevin was so moved by compassion that he kept his hand raised and palm open until the baby bird had fully hatched; and so, he is often depicted with a blackbird in his hand.

The legend of this Celtic saint is one that speaks deeply to a sense of kinship with creation. The Irish poet Seamus Heaney wrote a poem titled "St. Kevin and the Blackbird" in which he writes: "Kevin feels the warm eggs, the small breast, the tucked / Neat head and claws and, finding himself linked / Into the network of eternal life." According to tradition, St. Kevin had many other encounters with animals. For instance, it is said that an otter would sometimes bring him salmon from the lake so he could eat.

Our week on sacred rhythms brought us more in touch with how the cycles of the day, the month, and the year can offer us profound wisdom for our inner monk and artist. This week we focus on nature as a source of revelation, in particular on God's creatures. Helen Waddell's *Beasts and Saints* is filled with stories of saints from the Western monastic tradition (including the desert, Celtic, and Benedictine traditions), who had encounters with animals. Special connections and relationships to animals were once a sign of holiness.

In *The Dialogues of Gregory the Great,* which describes the life of St. Benedict, the author depicts how Benedict once was sent poisoned bread. Each day, a crow would visit Benedict to receive bread from him, and on this particular day he asked the crow to take the poisoned loaf far away so that it would not injure anyone. For this reason, St. Benedict is often depicted with a raven by his side.

In one of his letters, Thomas Merton describes the ideal monastic life: "The monk here and now is supposed to be living the life of the new creation in which right relation to all the rest of God's creatures is fully restored." The poet Kenneth Jackson wrote of the hermits: "The woodland birds might sing to him around his cell, but through it all, rarely expressed, always implicit, is the understanding that the bird and hermit are joining together in an act of worship; to him the very existence of nature was a song of praise in which he himself took part by entering into harmony with nature" (*Studies in Early Celtic Nature Poetry*).

When I go for my morning walk, I try to hold in my heart this image of joining together with the pigeons and the squirrels in the praise of creation. I am present to the trees and the crows as my *abbas* and *ammas,* my wisdom fathers and mothers. I sometimes ask for a word as I walk, and I listen for what is spoken to me. Creation is the foundation of my spiritual community, the matrix from which all of my work and loving are made possible. I remember that nature is the primary expression of divine artistry and that my commitment to the act of creating is in kinship with the world around me.

Each time you go for your walk, see if you can begin with a sense that you are stepping into a landscape that is animate and alive. We have separated ourselves from creation by claiming consciousness only for ourselves. Creation is the first scripture, offering wisdom to us with each turn. Claiming our inner monk means remembering that we are the children of the earth, and the earth is in our bodies. The rhythm we discover outside is also within. Remember the way that the breath offers us a microcosm of the seasons of each day and year.

Nature as Icon Space

If what a tree or a bush does is lost on you,
You are surely lost.

—DAVID WAGONER

Nature is a holy text for me, an icon, a window to the Divine Presence at work in the world. Just as we spend time gazing upon an icon or our beloved, we can also allow our gaze to be drawn to this most holy and splendid of sights. I can spend hours meditating with ocean waves lapping the shore, contemplating the ancient witness of grand red cedar trees, delighting in geese flying in patterns of support.

Gazing is an act of loving reverence, a perspective that opens me up to transformation. Icon spaces invite me to linger, to relish, to admire. I imagine those ancient poets who wrote the psalms of creation, celebrating God's grandeur and mystery. When I do so, I feel connected to my spiritual ancestors.

Nature is an icon that slowly shifts beneath my gaze, revealing a God who is constantly creating. From this viewpoint, I become aware of a holy presence, the Great Artist, at work in the world around me, and I begin to connect deeply to the divine at work within me, crafting and shaping my life, inviting me here this day to sit in stillness and witness to the beauty of the world.

Nature can teach us a great deal about creative rhythms and the elaborate use of color. Consider allowing nature to become a holy teacher on the artist's path. Pay attention to her artistic exuberance as an encouragement for your own flowering and experimentation. Notice how the dark stillness of night gives way to the burgeoning brilliance of sky in the morning. Consider how your own expression of dark and light through art reflects these primary forces.

Contemplative Practices

Invitation

Your invitation this week is to spend significant time in nature. It might be your backyard or a nearby park or a hiking trail. Allow this time to restore your contemplative and creative spirit. Be present to the ways the community of nature supports you in your monk and artist paths. Notice how creation is calling you to embrace these more deeply, and take time to reflect in your journal.

Lectio Divina

Psalm 104 is one of the great hymns of creation's praise found in the scriptures. I invite you to pray this text with lectio divina as a way of listening for the deeper invitation to your own relationship to creation. Bring this passage outside and pray with it under a tree or sitting in the grass. You might consider breaking it down into three or four sections and praying with it over a few days.

> *Bless the Lord, O my soul. O Lord my God, you are very great. You are clothed with honor and majesty,*
> *wrapped in light as with a garment. You stretch out the heavens like a tent,*
> *you set the beams of your chambers on the waters, you make the clouds your chariot,*

you ride on the wings of the wind,
you make the winds your messengers, fire and flame your ministers.
You set the earth on its foundations, so that it shall never be
*   shaken.*
You cover it with the deep as with a garment; the waters stood
*   above the mountains.*
You make springs gush forth in the valleys; they flow between the
*   hills,*
giving drink to every wild animal; the wild asses quench their
*   thirst.*
By the streams the birds of the air have their habitation; they sing
*   among the branches.*
From your lofty abode you water the mountains; the earth is
*   satisfied with the fruit of your work.*
You cause the grass to grow for the cattle, and plants for people to
*   use, to bring forth food from the earth,*
and wine to gladden the human heart, oil to make the face shine,
and bread to strengthen the human heart.
The trees of the Lord are watered abundantly, the cedars of
*   Lebanon that he planted.*

*—*Psalm 104:1–6, 10–16

Reflection Questions

- When you spend time outside this week, contemplate nature as the Creator's art. What does the work of the Divine Artist have to teach you about creativity and the creative process?
- Where have you discovered the overflowing fecundity of the world this week? What has the silence of creation whispered to you? What do the wind and earth have to say to you?

Visual Art Exploration

Creating Spontaneous Nature Altars and Mandalas

This week, take your camera with you on a contemplative walk. Go to a park or to the shore—somewhere you can experience the gifts of trees and rocks and water. Begin by focusing on your breath and entering into this experience with holy awareness and openness. Bring your awareness to your heart center and allow your gaze on the world around you to come from this heart space. The eyes of the heart receive the world with gentleness, openness, and sacred awe.

As you walk gather stones, twigs, leaves, shells—any object you encounter that catches your eye and invites you to spend time with it. This isn't about accumulating things, but about reverently receiving holy symbols. As you lift each one, offer a prayer or blessing of gratitude for the abundant gifts of creation.

Pause occasionally to create a spontaneous altar in the grass or along the edge of the path, either with the materials you have gathered or ones nearby. Consider laying out the sacred objects in the form of a *mandala*, which is the Sanskrit word for "circle." This circular shape can be found across traditions—in rose windows, illuminated texts, labyrinths, and in the *mandalas* Buddhist monks create from colored sand. Then allow your objects to blow away in the wind to practice detachment. The art you are creating in this process is temporary, a momentary gathering of prayers and offerings in celebration of nature's beauty.

Create a cairn. A cairn is a pile of stones to mark a pathway or indicate a site of importance, a sort of altar. Draw words or shapes in the sand or dirt with a twig. Pay attention to your inner movements and how you intuitively feel drawn to create. Notice what happens inside of you as you form shapes. Allow each creation to be its own altar celebrating the sacred presence found in nature. Notice if the cairn is an offering for something in particular—a person in your life, an event. Be present to the memories that rise up and want to be honored. When I spend time in nature, I am often drawn to remembering people in my life who have died as I connect to the sense of a "thin place," which the Celts described as any place where heaven and earth seem to come closer.

As you move through this process of creating *mandalas* and cairns, consider taking photos of each one. Or if it feels more appropriate, take time to create until the whole experience feels complete and then see if any of the creations want to be preserved by the camera lens as a witness.

Poetry Writing Exploration

A Psalm of Praise

Psalm 104 is a celebration of the glories of creation. This week consider writing your own psalm of praise in response to your time spent outdoors. The psalms are prayers and songs written to God. You might take the words of Psalm 104 as your starting point and rewrite it to express your own experience, or you might want to begin completely anew. Allow each line to be a tribute to the Original Artist and the ways you discover creativity at work in the world around you.

There is a general structure for praise psalms in scripture. They begin with a "call to praise," which is a declaration of God's abundant goodness and a call to the community to celebrate the Creator.

This is followed by reasons to praise God, such as the fecundity of creation and the ways we are supported in our flourishing by all of the elements of nature. The praise may also focus on how God has helped an individual or an entire community.

The psalm closes with a renewed call to praise in light of these examples listed. This is usually a repetition of the opening call, but it takes into account the poetic journey of gratitude that has been undertaken in the psalm.

> **Quick feather, still slate, deep bone**
> *I am like a river*
> *I carry the last snowfall of winter away to springtime*
> *Quick and still and deep*
> *In springtime, I carry violet dreamings to the sea*
> *I carry the last snowfall of winter away to springtime*
> *I offer gifts of feather, slate and bone*
> *In springtime, I carry dreams of violets to the sea*

Trees drink deeply
I bring gifts—feather and slate and bone
Quick and still and deep
Trees drink deeply
I am like a river

—MELINDA SCHWAKHOFER

SIMPLICITY: CREATIVE ASCETICISM *and* LEARNING WHEN *to* LET GO

Simplicity and Holy Asceticism

Simplicity is the seedbed for sane, free, illumined holy living.

—TILDEN EDWARDS

In the tradition of Christian monasticism, monks often take on extreme forms of ascetical practice as a path toward holiness and connection with the divine. We could unearth a great deal of theology and history behind this drive to go to extremes in a quest for a spiritual experience or out of a suspicion (or outright disdain) of the body and pleasure. Many such extremes and the thinking underlying them should be rejected. But rather than throwing asceticism out altogether, I invite you this week to consider the ways you are invited, as monks and artists, to a healthy and holy asceticism. How might we reclaim this life-giving practice in our complex and consumer-oriented lives in ways that free us for greater creativity, compassion, and service?

Asceticism essentially refers to the practice of paring down the external trappings of our lives to create more internal freedom. Our pace of life is killing us, and our lifestyles are slowly killing the environment in which we live. Simplicity calls us to live more intentionally. It also calls us to recognize life's essentials and what should be abandoned because of the unproductive energy it requires. We might discard thoughts, habits, or tangible objects that drain energy from our hearts' truest desires.

Consider how you are called to a holy and healthy asceticism. As monks and artists, how might we reclaim this life-giving practice in our complex, consumer-oriented lives to free us for greater creativity, compassion, and service?

When we live simply, we relinquish expectations for how things will or should be, and remain present to the way things really are. We bring a contemplative presence to the world, compassionate and curious about what we might discover. Simplicity opens wide the doors for a process of letting go, allowing us to be fully present to the graces given us in this precise moment.

When we practice simplicity, we also learn to dispose of burdens in our lives. These might be possessions, opinions, expectations, or commitments that no longer feed us but that we continue to fulfill because of how we want to appear to others. Simplicity invites us to make choices about our priorities and how we want to expend our limited energy. What are the commitments that keep us from making time for creating art or writing? How often do we set aside the joy of creative expression because we are "too busy"? When we are able to acknowledge what needs to be released, our vision expands, and we can become grateful for what is given in each moment. This gratitude expands our hearts so that we may receive the world as gift.

Spaciousness

A thousand half-loves must be surrendered to take a whole heart home.

—RUMI

Take a moment to breathe deeply and exhale with a heavy sigh. Try this a couple of times and experience inner spaciousness. Then reach your arms wide around you, exploring each direction, stretching your finger-tips out into space and savoring the expanse around you.

In his article "Entering the Emptiness," Gerald May writes:

> Space is freedom from confinement, from preoccupation, from oppression, from drivenness, and from all the other interior and exterior forces that bind and restrict our spirits. We need space in the first place simply to recognize how compelled and bound we are. Then we need space to allow the compulsions to ease and the bonds to loosen. To the extent that space is permitted by grace and our own will-ingness, we discover expanding emptiness in which conse-cration can happen, room for love to make its home in us.

This sense of space can be discovered through contemplative living. Rather than running to and from appointments and meetings in a breath-less and endless succession of adrenaline-releasing activities, contempla-tives allow time to be present between commitments. In doing so, we can live more intentionally and thoughtfully. When each movement has meaning and purpose, then each moment is filled with a holy charge of energy. We then create an inner spaciousness. Consider three aspects of the spaciousness that May describes:

Spaciousness of Form: physical, geographic spaces like the wide-open expanse of fields, water, and sky and the welcoming simplicity of uncluttered room; closets that contain only that which is necessary; care-fully chosen art that reflects who we truly are.

Explore the places where you are addicted to filling up space, where you are drawn to eradicate any emptiness. Consider what you want to let go of to create more physical space.

Spaciousness of Time: pauses in our day when we are freed from tasks, agendas, and other demands; time to simply sink into the spaciousness offered to us; moments when we touch the eternal and lose track of all time.

Again, notice if there is an impulse to fill your time with nonessentials as a means to avoid what spaciousness might reveal to you. Gerald May suggests that our busyness is an expression of our "addiction to fulfillment," leaving little room "for love to make its home in us." Consider what commitments you want to let go of to create more space in your daily life.

Spaciousness of Soul: the inner emptiness; the cave of the heart.

Depending upon how we meet this soul space, we may experience it as either open possibility or void and nothingness; as creative potential or dulling boredom; as quiet, peaceful eternity or as restless yearning for fulfillment. This inner spaciousness is expressed in the Latin phrase *vacare Deo,* which means to be "free for God." True spaciousness of the soul is having the will and courage to experience things as they are. We eliminate the expectations we bring to a moment and allow ourselves to witness what is present and absorb any wisdom we might receive. Consider the inner expectations and voices you want to let go of to create more interior space.

For many years, I resisted beginning a new project until the physical space was cleared. I used to think this was my way of procrastinating. Finally one day, I allowed myself to embrace this clearing and organizing work as a central part of my creative process. Putting away old projects and files and organizing what was needed for the new project became about intentionally filing away the old and making space for the new. It became a part of my ritual for creative expression and made the process easier.

Revisit the ritual and blessing you created in week one for beginning your creative time. Consider creating a ritual of transition as you move between creative works. How do you honor what has been completed and brought to fruition? How do you make space for what new expressions will be emerging? Are there poems or other readings which would help to support you in bringing intention to these moments of transition?

Sacred Yes and No

*By the sacred yes or sacred no I mean that affir-
mation or negation that comes from a deep
place of wisdom and courage, even if it creates
conflict or disagreement. The sacred yes is not
willful or egocentric, but rather is willing and
surrendered. The sacred no is not rebellion or
refusal, but always the necessary protecting of
boundaries.*

—RICHARD ROHR

In Jungian studies there is a recognition that we contain within us a
feminine and masculine dimension to our souls. These dimensions each
express different qualities. The feminine dimension with its archetype of
welcoming, nurturing, enfolding energy (such as the Mother) is the sacred
yes of our lives—the things, people, and opportunities we embrace.

The masculine dimension with its archetype of boundary setting and
protection (such as the Warrior) is the sacred no of our lives—the healthy
setting of limits and protectors of our gifts and energies so we don't over-
extend ourselves.

Every time we say "yes" to something in our lives, we are also saying (often unconsciously) "no" to something else. In other words, each
time we commit energy to projects or people, we take energy away from
something else. When we bring conscious awareness to this truth, we can
commit with more intention.

There is a connection between the sacred yes and no, and the rhythms
of the breath and seasons. For example, inhaling is parallel to spring
and dawn, the breathing in of new life and new beginnings. The space
between inhaling and exhaling is parallel to summer or day, that moment
of experiencing life's fullness. These are the times of the sacred yes, when
life is full of blossoming and fruit and invitation.

Exhaling can be compared to autumn or dusk, when we consider endings and surrender. And the pause between exhaling and inhaling is like
the night of winter, that time of being in between, when we dwell in darkness and are uncertain of what the next breath will bring. These are the

moments of the sacred no, when we consider what needs letting go and the ways we need to nurture ourselves.

Contemplative Practices

Invitation

Declutter your life and begin again with a sense of renewal and clarity. Notice what you can release to make more space. External, physical shifts often have an internal impact as well. Contemplate the commitments in your life and ponder where you are being called to utter the sacred "yes" and sacred "no." Choose one area to focus on, perhaps a physical space such as your office or a relational space where you are experiencing dynamics that are difficult.

Lectio Divina

Sheri Hostetler's poem that follows is a marvelous reminder of the ultimate simplicity of our lives: that essentially we do not own anything; we are only brief visitors in this world. It is an invitation to humility as well, to remember our mortality and to allow that awareness to shape our relationship to the things we feel attached to. It isn't that possessions are bad; it is that it takes energy to maintain them or avoid dealing with them. Engage in lectio divina with this poem and listen for an invitation to simplicity emerging from your prayer.

Instructions
Give up the world; give up self; finally, give up God.
Find god in rhododendrons and rocks,
passers-by, your cat.
Pare your beliefs, your absolutes.
Make it simple; make it clean.
No carry-on luggage allowed.
Examine all you have
with a loving and critical eye, then
throw away some more.

Repeat. Repeat.
Keep this and only this:
    what your heart beats loudly for
    what feels heavy and full in your gut.
There will only be one or two
things you will keep,
and they will fit lightly
in your pocket.

—SHERI HOSTETLER

Reflection Questions

- What does healthy asceticism look like for you? How do your inner monk and artist invite you into greater simplicity of commitment and practice? What is enough for this season of your life?
- When you contemplate greater interior and exterior freedom, how do you experience these in your body?
- How does space play a role in your artistic creativity? What do you notice about your needs for your surroundings when you move into creative time? What are the possessions, commitments, and expectations that distract you from being fully present? Can you lay these aside altogether or create a way to symbolically set them aside for the time of holy birthing ahead?
- When you connect with your own place of deep wisdom and courage, what are the *sacred yes* and *sacred no* that arise? What are you being called to welcome more fully and to embrace? Where are you being called to create stronger boundaries for self-care and nurturing? What are the commitments you have made which take energy away from your deepest yes? What are the fierce aspects of yourself that can help you to clarify what is life-draining and what you need to release to live fully and to help maintain boundaries?
- When you connect with your own deep wisdom and courage, what are the *sacred yes* and *sacred no* that arise? What are you being called to welcome more fully and to embrace? Where are you being called to create stronger boundaries for self-care and nurturing? What are the commitments that take energy away from your deepest yes?

Visual Art and Writing Exploration

A Stop-Doing List and a To-Be List

Materials needed: paper, markers in different colors.

Do you make lots of to-do lists? I write them all the time—almost every day. I create a list of my priorities for that day. It is a helpful practice and keeps me focused on what is most important, but sometimes I become overwhelmed when the number of tasks on my list is clearly greater than my capacity to complete them. I love crossing something off my list—until I have to add something else. And sometimes I long to release the desire to have a list at all and just enter into the heartbeat of the day.

Consider making two different lists:

The first is a stop-doing list. What are the activities, habits, thoughts, etc., that take energy away from your true calling?

The second is a to-be list. What are the ways of being in the world you want to cultivate? What are the practices that help to nurture and sustain these?

Begin by grounding yourself and connecting to your breath. Approach this art exploration through the heart, opening yourself to what the process might reveal to you. Enter into the delight of discovery and allow this time to be a prayer.

Using markers, write "stop doing" on top of one sheet of paper and "to be" on top of another. Give yourself about ten minutes to create each list, allowing yourself to just write without thinking. Respond from the heart and let your intuition guide you. Do not shy away from puzzling or surprising words that arise. The colored markers help to make this a more playful and intuitive experience than if you were to simply write or type words on a page. Allow yourself some playfulness and add colorful flourishes, designs, and borders around your words.

When you are done, take some time to be present to what has emerged. Notice how you are feeling in response and reflect on the process. Consider posting these lists in a prominent place, perhaps by your desk or computer.

Movement and Voice Exploration

Sacred Yes and No

This exercise needs to be done when you have some time alone, or at least can close the door and let your partner or children know that there may be sounds coming from the room, but you are okay and do not want to be disturbed. Consider recording the instructions into a voice recorder so that you do not have to refer back and forth to the book. At the very least, read through the instructions a couple of times to get a sense of what the exercise invites you to engage through your body and voice.

You might want to play reflective music (or keep it silent if it is more inviting) and allow yourself time to explore in movement. Through shape and gesture, express your sacred yes with your body. Begin by grounding yourself by feeling your feet on the floor and bending your knees. Connect to the rhythm of your breath. Gently draw your awareness from your head to your heart. When you feel ready, begin to move. Don't think this through; allow your body to teach you how to embody your sacred yes. Take time to play. Explore a variety of shapes and movements, until you find the one that serves as a gesture of welcome and embrace. Add your voice to this experience if you feel the pull—you might just shape the word "yes" with your mouth—or allow the words to emerge in the form of a song that rises up from within you. Again, allow space to experiment with this. Rest in this experience of movement and voice for a while, noticing where you experience the sacred yes in your body and the feelings that rise up, simply making room for them and witnessing your inner process.

Take time to journal anything you noticed and reflect on your life commitments. To what in your life do you want to sing this embracing yes?

Then shift to another piece of music, one with more strength to it—less mellow, more assertive. You can also do this without music if silence feels more powerful. Connect with your breath again, and move your awareness into your heart. Explore in movement, shape, and gesture how your body longs to express the sacred no. Again, don't think this through but allow your body to teach you how to bring the sacred no into your whole being. Breathe in a sense of fierceness and protection of boundaries. Imagine there is something precious you are being called to guard (which is, in fact, true). Experiment with a variety of shapes and movements until you find one that feels satisfying as a fierce movement of enclosure or resistance. Add your voice again to this experience if you feel the pull—saying "no," then shouting "no," snarling, growling, then perhaps stomping your feet and throwing your entire body into vocalizing the "no." Repeat this a few times and notice where you experience this in your body and what feelings rise up, making room for whatever emerges. Return to journaling again, reflecting on your observations and the life commitments that come to mind as you utter this powerful sacred "no." If specific things come to mind for you, experiment with saying "no" to them in this forceful way, bringing your whole body to the experience.

At the end of this experience, experiment with switching between the sacred yes and the sacred no, allowing each one to have some space in your body, honoring the way they support each other. Notice which one is more comfortable and welcoming and which one stirs your own resistance. Invite both aspects to have their full presence within you. Imagine your inner monk and your inner artist joining you in this sacred yes and sacred no as well.

Take time following this exercise to journal and reflect on what you noticed and discovered.

> ***today i will . . .***
> *today i will give my desire for*
> *permanence the day off*
> *and sit in a chapel*
> *made of twigs and spit*
> *today i will give my desire for*
> *certainty the day off*
> *and dwell in the place*
> *of not-knowing*
> *today i will give my desire for*
> *security the day off,*
> *open the windows and*
> *let in the breath of fresh air*
>
> —STACY STALL WILLS

CREATIVE WORK *as* VOCATION *and* HOLY SERVICE

Mindful Work

I want to be with people who submerge
in the task . . .
The work of the world is common as mud . . .
But the thing worth doing well done
has a shape that satisfies, clean and evident.

—Marge Piercy

Work is fundamental and necessary and physi-
cal and holy and spiritual and creative. Work,
you see, is a basic part of the monastic tradition.

—Joan Chittister

When they live by the labor of their hands, as our
ancestors and the apostles did,
then they are really monastics.

—Rule of St. Benedict, 48:8

In week three, we explored how the *Rule of St. Benedict* calls us to regard all the tools of the monastery as sacred vessels of the altar. Each plate and fork is holy; each object that serves us is worthy of reverence. In week four, we explored the hours of the day as a call to be present to the unfolding rhythm of the seasons and to remember that God is with us in each moment. In a monastic approach to work, we are called to extend this sacred awareness to everything we do, including our labors.

In the *Rule*, St. Benedict mentions that the monks should "not be downcast" if they need to gather the harvest. In St. Benedict's time, much of the monk's labor was considered to be the work of slaves. And yet everyone who came to the monastery, whether wealthy or poor, shared equally in the labor. Benedict pointed out that persons truly became monks when they lived from the work of their hands as the apostles did.

Benedict always considered work as a holy gift. The act of earning one's daily food and shelter was seen as an honorable task. Not all work feels meaningful—some of it may feel more like drudgery. And not everything that is considered work is paid labor. Even if we have a job we love, we still need to do dishes and laundry and clean the bathroom. Sometimes we have work we dread and still have to come home to the tasks of daily living. Some of us take care of children or aging parents as full-time work or in addition to our day jobs.

However, just as the desert mothers and fathers remind us that our cells can teach us everything, so can our daily work be a place of inner transformation. The call of the monk is to bring absolute attention to the work at hand. When we lose this attention, we also lose our freedom. When we spend our time wishing we were doing something else, we forget that the sacred is right in our midst. Ralph Waldo Emerson wrote: "Sufficient to today are the duties of today." You are called to "spend yourself on the work before you; / well assured that the right performance of this hour's duties / will be the best preparation." When performing an assignment, the monk is invited to be satisfied with the task at hand. Part of the contemplative path is recognizing that growth happens in any context and that any situation in which we find ourselves can offer the fullness of grace.

In *Music of Silence*, Benedictine monk David Steindl-Rast and Sharon Lebell offer this invitation:

> Work, if we don't approach it consciously, will suck us into
> its demands. Then we become slaves, no matter how high
> up we are on the ladder. . . . Even people who have jobs they
> don't like and find meaningless can still be free within them
> . . . by reminding themselves deliberately and often, why
> they do them. As long as we do work out of love for those
> whom we love, we do it for a good reason. Love is the best
> reason for our labors. Love makes what we do and suffer
> rise like music, like a soaring line of chant.

Even work that feels creative and rises from our call to be artists involves periods of challenging intensity. As a writer, I always find the editing process one of the most difficult aspects of the work, and yet I also recognize it as one of the most valuable. Writing feels like grace most days, flowing with ease. When I feel blocked, often a long walk or time spent cooking is enough to shift something open. Otherwise I will engage the block in dialogue as an act of inner hospitality. To do so, I imagine having a conversation with the part of myself feeling blocked and ask it to tell me what it needs and wants from me. The experience with my resistance is part of my own inner transformation. As I listen for what the work needs in this stage and how it wants to come to birth in the world, I discover my own places that need releasing or ways to express my ideas with more clarity.

Consider the tasks in your life that you do grudgingly. Maybe you dislike your job, have to care for a home and family, or are responsible for other ordinary life demands. Then try to remember why you do the work. Do you work for love's sake? Are there ways to love challenges and to reframe them so that they rise like music and lift up your creative heart as Steindl-Rast and Lebell suggest?

What is the love that calls you to your labors in the world? Do you need to maintain a job to earn a living? Does this work support your ability to also create and rest and dream? Does it offer shelter and nourishment to the people you love, including yourself? How might you bring more love and delight to all of the tasks to which you are called?

Work as Vocation

Work: an opportunity for discovering and shaping; the place where self meets the world.

—DAVID WHYTE

And although God is the artist, and each created being bears God's mark, the work of the soul's unfolding is a co-creative labor involving each person as a participant with God.

—NORVENE VEST

Our daily work may rise out of our true calling in the world, or it may just pay the bills; either way, we each have a vocation. We each were given certain gifts to offer in service to others. Our calling is deeply connected to our creativity. The truths we long to express in the world and the way we feel moved to give form to beauty are signs of the Spirit at work within us. Vocation is a daily invitation to be fully who we are and to allow our lives to unfold in ways that are organic to this deepest identity.

Multiple biblical figures received new names from God because of how they responded to the holy invitation burning in their hearts. Abram becomes Abraham; Sarai becomes Sarah, Jacob becomes Israel, Simon becomes Peter, and Saul becomes Paul. Each has a transformative encounter with God, takes the risk to respond, and is marked by God's grace in a particular way that leads to his or her unfolding journey. "I will give . . . a white stone, and on the white stone is written a new name that no one knows except the one who receives it" (Rv 2:17). Our vocation is written deep in our hearts, and only we can say what it is.

In his *Rule*, St. Benedict emphasizes the spiritual life as a movement of call and response: "What could be sweeter to us than this voice of the Lord inviting us?" (*Rule of St. Benedict,* Prologue 19). God is always inviting us to deeper relationship and wholeness. In this growing intimacy with the sacred presence in our lives, we also become more united with our unique call in the world. As we respond to God's offerings, we discover more deeply how we are to live our lives in their fullness.

Mary Oliver describes the heart of vocation in her poem "The Messenger." She writes that her work is "loving the world" and goes on to say, "Let me / keep my mind on what matters, / which is my work, / which is mostly standing still and learning to be / astonished." Vocation is not necessarily a particular task or path. More often it is a way of bringing our vocations into our jobs. How might your relationship to work be transformed if you saw your vocation as offering as much compassion as possible, no matter the details of the actual work? Or, as an artist, consider how you might bring creativity and imagination to the smallest, most ordinary of tasks.

Your call to cultivate your inner monk and artist is a response to your vocation. This is the prayer God is already praying within you and asking you to join wholeheartedly. When we offer ourselves to this work, our prayer becomes an act of consent, a yes to our gifts.

Work as Co-creative

In Benedictine spirituality, work is what we do to continue what God wanted done. Work is co-creative. Keeping a home that is beautiful and ordered and nourishing and artistic is co-creative. Working in a machine shop that makes gears for tractors is co-creative. Working in an office that processes loan applications for people who are trying to make life more humane is co-creative. . . . We work because the world is unfinished and it is ours to develop. We work with a vision in mind. . . . Work is a commitment to God's service.

—JOAN CHITTISTER

Human work is the primary way we care for the world given to us by the Creator. Through work we help to usher in the unfolding of God's reign among us. We also cultivate ways of seeing this reality already present among us. Our attention to compassion and creativity is a commitment to laboring alongside the Divine Worker in bringing about a more just and beautiful world. The work is so large that we may be tempted to despair or abandon our part, but humility reminds us to honor our gifts and limits. We are called to be proactive and to bring our whole hearts to the task, trusting that a greater source than ourselves weaves those tasks together.

Consider how your perspective might change if you realized that the world needs what you have to offer. Monastic spirituality reminds us that God invites each one of us in every moment to respond to our unique call. One of the things I love most about lectio divina is the way a group of people can read the same scripture passage at the same time in prayer together, and yet each person will have a unique experience and response to a call that is specific to the reader's life circumstances. The same is true with how we are each called to share gifts in the world.

In traditional monasticism, monks dedicate their whole lives to the practice. They do not marry or have family lives. Nor do they have jobs outside of their community. The vast increase in the number of oblates, especially in the last several years, witnesses to a new energy rising. New questions are being asked about how to live monasticism in ordinary ways. What does it mean to be a monk in the world? How are we called to regard our work from a monastic perspective? How might we still bring this wholehearted dedication to the practice of contemplative ways of being?

Contemplative Practices

Invitation

Contemplate how you are called to work in the world and how you might focus on the tasks you labor through. Consider offering a prayer or blessing each time you begin your work, simply asking that your work is the fullest expression possible of how God is calling you to offer your gifts to the world. You are also invited to spend some time listening for the deeper voice of vocation and considering if God is offering you a new name.

Lectio Divina

In *Friend of the Soul*, Norvene Vest translates the first line of the following passage from the *Rule of St. Benedict* to mean that work is the "friend of the soul." Engage with these words through lectio divina and see what invitation emerges.

> Idleness is the enemy of the soul. Therefore, the brothers should have specified periods for manual labor as well as for prayerful reading. . . . When they live by the labor of their hands, as our fathers and the apostles did, then they are really monks. Yet, all things are to be done with moderation on account of the fainthearted. (48:1, 8–9)

Reflection Questions

- What are the joys and challenges you find in your daily work?
- How might considering your vocation as a daily calling transform how you view your work in the world?
- In what ways do small tasks done with great love contribute to co-creation with God and the unfolding of a more just and loving world?

Guided Meditation

Bringing a Heart of Compassion

Our coworkers, supervisors, clients, and customers are often the most challenging aspect of our work. This week's meditation is an adaptation from a Buddhist meditation practice of loving kindness. It invites you to bring a heart of compassion to all those with whom you work.

Find a comfortable position and become aware of your body. Notice your body's delights and discomforts and shift in any way that brings more ease to you physically. Focus on your breath, noticing its natural rhythm. Gently deepen this cycle, and as you breathe in, receive this life-nourishing gift; and as you breathe out, release any tension in your body or your mind. Spend a few moments being present to your breath.

Allow your breath to draw your attention from your head down to your heart center. Observe what you are feeling right now, letting the truth of your experience to have room within you without trying to change it. Then draw into your awareness the infinite compassion of God, which the mystics tell us resides in our hearts. Allow the air you inhale to fill your experience and feelings with this compassion. When you exhale, release any judgments or hesitancies that block you from this compassion. For this moment in time, remember that you are enough and that God created you whole and holy.

Repeat the words of the Buddhist meditation to yourself. (There are many variations of this, so consider writing words that speak most deeply to your heart.)

> May I be peaceful, may I be happy, may I be healthy.
> May I be free of suffering, may I be at ease.
> May I know I am loved, may I be safe.

Focus on someone you care deeply about, like a good friend. Embrace a sense of that person's presence and then breathe in deeply, remembering the infinite source of compassion dwelling within you. As you exhale imagine the compassion filling your friend or loved one. Address the following prayer to him or her:

> May you be peaceful, may you be happy, may you be healthy.
> May you be free of suffering, may you be at ease.
> May you know you are loved, may you be safe.
> Rest in this loving awareness for a few moments.

Call to mind someone you know who is struggling right now. Embrace the person's presence and breathe deeply again. With your exhaling, imagine sending compassion to him or her. Repeat the prayer and rest in this space.

Now think of a person with whom you don't have an emotional connection, a neutral figure like the grocery store clerk or bank teller. As you call this person's presence to you, take another deep breath. As you exhale, imagine that you are breathing out compassion and sending it to the person. Offer the prayer again.

Focus on someone with whom you experience hostility or anger— perhaps a coworker or supervisor. Embrace the person's presence and breathe this infinite source of compassion into his or her being and repeat the prayer. Rest in this experience, noticing what it stirs in you.

In the last movement of this meditation, imagine your heart expanding in all directions, embracing all people and all creatures, sending compassion and offering the prayer on their behalf. Meditate on this image.

Gather your energy back into your heart and offer an intention to bring this compassionate awareness to all of the tasks of your day. Then gently allow your breath to bring you again to the room and return to your day slowly, carrying this experience with you.

Visual Art Exploration

Writing Your New Name on a Stone

Earlier, we explored the scriptural tradition of God offering a new name to those who have listened and responded to God's call. We are nearing the end of our journey together through this material. Consider if God is calling you to embrace a new name through this commitment to your creative and contemplative soul. You may be called to a new identity rather than a new name. Perhaps you have been able to embrace the name of monk or artist more deeply for yourself.

Take a contemplative walk this week somewhere you are likely to find stones—by a river or beach, in a forest—or perhaps you already have a stone that feels meaningful. If you want to find a white stone, you could even visit a landscaping or gardening store, remembering that these are sacred places as well, and seek out the stone that feels satisfying. Hold it in your hand and notice its shape and texture and weight. Stones are sacred symbols of the earth. Recall how cairns are human markers of significant places or tools to provide direction or a path.

Once you find the right stone for this process, take time to be present to the name you want to claim. When it has emerged, use paint or a permanent marker to write your new name on the stone. Place the stone on your altar and allow it to be a daily reminder of this deepened commitment to embrace the fullness of your vocation. Consider holding it in your hand each morning before you begin your work to remind yourself of your calling in the world.

Poetry Writing Exploration

How to Be a Poet: Writing a Poem of Instruction

This poem by Wendell Berry is considered a poem of instruction. It is written to remind both writer and reader how to perform a task. This week, consider writing your own poem of instruction for what you want to remember when you approach your work, which could be your day job, or the process of maintaining a home, or your work as an artist or writer in the world. What are the qualities and tasks that ground you in a sense of the sacred presence pulsing through everything you do?

> **How to be a Poet**
> *(to remind myself)*
> *Make a place to sit down.*
> *Sit down. Be quiet.*
> *You must depend upon*
> *affection, reading, knowledge,*
> *skill—more of each*
> *than you have—inspiration,*
> *work, growing older, patience,*
> *for patience joins time*
> *.to eternity. Any readers*
> *who like your work,*
> *doubt their judgment.*
> *Breathe with unconditional breath*
> *the unconditioned air.*
> *Shun electric wire.*

Communicate slowly. Live
a three-dimensioned life;
stay away from screens.
Stay away from anything
that obscures the place it is in.
There are no unsacred places;
there are only sacred places
and desecrated places.
Accept what comes from silence.
Make the best you can of it.
Of the little words that come
out of the silence, like prayers
prayed back to the one who prays,
make a poem that does not disturb
the silence from which it came.

—WENDELL BERRY

Let this poem be your inspiration for your own poem-writing experience.

Twelve Stones

I restack them again at this new beginning
Pink and gray granite from a place I went to school
A red, sandstone pancake from the beach of my first solo holiday
Marbled quartz pocketed on a lion walk in southern Africa
Shale from a Long Walk to Freedom up Table Mountain
A thinking stone from Bowen Island on my fortieth
A limestone slab from a day-long conversation in Jasper National
        Park
Five smooth stones from the beach close to my Vancouver home
The shiny orange one, a gift bearing the name Creativity
Their presence marks the middle of each mini-miracle
Geographic sites of giant killing
Each one used to cross a Jordan

—LAUREL PRITCHARD

My journal is your sacred tablet
Colors, shapes, strokes, are my steppingstones to you
Day to Day—a practice in w-holy living
Others freshen my artistic openings
Colors, shapes, strokes, are my steppingstones to you

Our souls connect and are ignited by paint
Others freshen my artistic openings
My wake-up call is the blank page
Our souls connect and are united by paint
Day to day—a practice in w-holy living
My wake-up call is the blank page
My journal is your sacred tablet

—SUZIE MASSEY

CREATING *an* ARTIST'S RULE *of* LIFE

An Artist's Rule of Life

Creativity arises out of the tension between spontaneity and limitations, the latter—like the river banks—forcing the spontaneity into various forms which are essential to the work of art or poem.

—ROLLO MAY

Together we have explored the gifts of monastic wisdom for nurturing our creative soul. The insights here have been drawn from desert, Celtic, and Benedictine spirituality. The *Rule of St. Benedict* is a wisdom guide for healthy and balanced living that also fosters creativity. The creative life requires this gentle tension between freedom and structure, or "spontaneity and limitations," as Rollo May says. This is the place where a rule of life can be helpful, providing a gentle trellis of structure for our lives. When approached with freedom and playfulness, boundaries can help spark our creativity. Take a moment to identify your own life boundaries.

Where have they been freeing and where have they been restrictive? What were the differences in those experiences?

As human beings seeking to live meaningful lives, we hunger for some kind of structure, a set of practices that challenge us and help us to grow. Yet, if our rule is too rigorous, we can become suffocated by legalism. The paradox of the spiritual life is that it needs a healthy balance of structure and freedom to thrive. This is the paradox of the creative process as well. When I teach workshops on the arts as a spiritual practice, I begin with more structured exercises to help gently guide participants into the experience. Then we can move to less structure and more improvised expression. Sometimes the blank canvas or page can be terrifying because of the complete freedom. Writing prompts or suggestions for visual expression or movement can give us a foundation and help us to connect with our creative energy while we move into greater and greater freedom. Commitment to regular writing or creative time is a discipline or practice that also helps to nurture creativity.

Beyond the creative act itself, I find that there are certain rhythms to my life that are essential for my creative energy. These include writing each morning, walking to care for my body, letting my energy shift out of my head for a while, knowing when to let go and let something incubate, and getting adequate rest and play. The balance of the Benedictine life is most conducive to my creative life. Of course, there are many other systems and traditions one could follow, and the purpose of the life rule is to grow in our awareness of the holy presence. If creativity is one of the ways in which we reflect the Creator, then a rule of life that nurtures our creativity is one that can also help us to grow spiritually.

A rule of life is essentially a commitment to specific practices you want to incorporate into your regular routine. A rule is meant to be balanced and not out of reach. It should not make you feel guilty for not living up to it, so aim for a rule of moderation. If you find the word "rule" difficult, you might imagine it as a trellis—a balance of structure and open space through which you can grow, offering boundaries while remaining open-ended and flexible. You do not have to write your once-and-for-all-forever rule of life. In fact, I encourage you to reflect regularly, perhaps at each transition to a new season, and notice whether your rule is providing too little or too much structure for you.

This week is an act of integration of all that has been previously discussed and a way to name the practices you want to commit to for this next season of your life. Allow some time to reflect on the theme of each week, noticing which aspects of the monastic path have felt the most nourishing and inviting. Make room for those aspects that were challenging as well, honoring how challenges can offer us wisdom for the inner journeys.

A rule of life is essentially a document that is broken down into several wide categories that encourage balance. So in creating your rule, you might consider some of the following questions:

- Which prayer practices nourish you? What would be a sustainable commitment to prayer for you daily, weekly, monthly, seasonally, annually?

- What are the ways you can commit to better integrating art into your everyday life? What are the support structures you need to make this happen?

- What commitments to yourself do you want to make? Where are your areas of further growth? Where would you like to deepen your practice? What are your growing edges, places where you long to be stretched beyond your current understanding, right now?

- What relationships in your life do you want to cultivate—relationships with self, family, friends, community, nature, global concerns, God? What commitments might you make to contribute to their flourishing? What has been the communal wisdom gleaned from this time?

- Revisit your inner monk and artist wisdom cards from week one and spend some time in reflection on the questions that were raised there. What new responses have been stirred during these twelve weeks?

- Consider again the commitments of stability, obedience, and conversion. How might your rule help you to integrate these commitments into your everyday life?

- How might your inner monk and artist guide the writing of your rule? What are they inviting you to consider as you move forward?

- What are the limitations of your life—what Rollo May called the riverbanks—that help nurture your creative expression, and what are the prisons that serve to squelch it? Where do you find the sparks that help to inspire you? Where do you desire to feel more freedom? Where do you need more support? What are the commitments you want to make right now in this season?

We come to the end of this book knowing that it is really just a beginning. St. Benedict wisely described his *Rule* as "a little rule for beginners." The vow of conversion reminds us that we are continually growing and stretching and discovering. The contemplative life is about an expansion of the heart. As we slow down to listen for the sacred whispers in each moment, both within and without, and as we grow in our capacity to hold our own feelings, we also grow in our capacity to love the world. Our role as artists is to give this form, to express our own deep love of the world, to call others to wonder and surprise, to stand in solidarity with those who suffer.

In his *Rule*, Benedict writes: "Your way of acting should be different from the world's way" (*Rule of St. Benedict*, 4:20). Claiming the path of monk and artist means witnessing to a different way of being in the world. We are called to live in ways that demonstrate the potential for compassion, the grace of presence, the revelation in each moment. This is a life lived on the edges of what the world values, and it is a challenging place to be. The edge is also that place of creative vitality, of remembering the God who is in this very moment creating something new. Living the life of a monk and artist in the world means we cultivate ways of being present to the dynamic creativity pulsing through our own veins. Our work calls us to offer this vision in service to the whole.

What *Must* You Do?

There is only one thing you should do. Go into yourself. Find out the reason that commands you to write; see whether it has spread its roots into the very depths of your heart; confess to yourself whether you would have to die if you were forbidden to write. This most of all: ask yourself in the most silent hour of your night: must I write? Dig into yourself for a deep answer. And if this answer rings out in assent, if you meet this solemn question with a strong, simple "I must," then build your life in accordance with this necessity; your whole life, even into its humblest and most indifferent hour, must become a sign and witness to this impulse.

—RAINER MARIA RILKE
LETTERS TO A YOUNG POET

In reading this book, you have undoubtedly discovered new invitations: practices that have nourished and enlivened you, ways to express your creative longings, and wide-open spaces within filled with holy possibility.

The quotation above from Rilke is one of my favorites, and I return to it often to remember the call to craft my life to support this deepest desire. As I grow older, I realize that I am wholly responsible for making my creative life a priority. No one else is going to ensure the time I need to embrace who I am. I rely on support from my friends and community, but ultimately I must listen each day for the holy invitation being whispered in quiet spaces and respond as best I can. Sometimes this means uttering a sacred "no" to very valuable activities.

In Rilke's *Letters to a Young Poet*, he writes of the poet's fundamental impulse to write. You could substitute any of your deep desires for the word "write." What in your life has spread its roots into the very depths of your heart? What must you do to be fully yourself? Is it something you are even ready to name? Speak it aloud, just for a moment, and allow those words to hum in the air around you, maybe even sing them aloud: "I am an artist . . . or a writer . . . or a dancer . . . or a monk . . . or . . ."

Is your life a sign and witness to this deepest desire? What would you need to change for this to be true? How could your rule support this fundamental call? Allow the writing of your rule to be an act of loving and generous support for this part of yourself that must exist.

Monk of the Deep Creative Imagination

Whenever I think of a monk today, I don't think of a Catholic monk or a Christian monk or a

Buddhist monk or a Zen monk, and I don't think
of male or female monks. I imagine the monk
as a spirit that engendered monasticism and
moves a certain few individuals to live that spir-
it as a way of life. For me, the more interesting
monk is a figure of the deep creative imagina-
tion, who can inspire anyone toward an experi-
ence of virtues and styles epitomized by monks
of all traditions.

—THOMAS MOORE
MEDITATIONS ON THE MONK WHO DWELLS IN DAILY LIFE

The monastic spirit and path is broader than any denomination or tradition. It is an expansive way of being in the world. I find I have much in common with the Buddhist monastic spirit. The monastic way opens us up to conversation with others through the lens of practice and experience. Being a monk in the world means that my life may inspire my neighbor, whether Christian or not, to live a life of greater presence and compassion. As a monk, I discover the sacred in all things, all persons, all experiences.

As we near the end of this journey, consider how as a monk you are rooted in an ancient set of practices that span traditions and cultures. As an artist, you come from a lineage of those who have offered creative vision in service to the world. What does being a monk of the "deep creative imagination" mean for you? How might your art and creativity inspire others to living a life of wholeness and integrity?

Contemplative Practices

Invitation

This final week of our process is a time of reflection, integration, and commitment. Consider ways an artist's rule of life can continue to help nourish your contemplative and creative practice.

Lectio Divina with Life Experience

Practice lectio divina with your experience, viewing your life as a sacred text. Begin by centering yourself. As you move into stillness, reflect on these last several weeks of working with the material in this book. Allow images, phrases, and insights to rise up, and be present to them briefly. This is a time of honoring what has happened.

As you continue to focus on your memories, notice if a particular word, phrase, or image stands out as a common theme. Spend a few minutes with this thought.

Enter into reflection, allowing this word, phrase, or image to unfold in your imagination. Pay attention to the images, feelings, or memories stirring in response and make internal space for them.

Once you have reflected for some time, recognize any invitations. When you think of your life story as a sacred text, do you find God calling you to a particular awareness or action? What are the things you most want to remember from this time? What do you carry forward with you? Be present to this sense of invitation, thinking how you might respond.

Close with inner stillness, releasing the words and images moving through you. Simply breathe in gratitude for what this experience has offered.

Visual Art and Writing Exploration

Rule of Life

> *Therefore we intend to establish a school for the Lord's service. In drawing up its regulations we hope to set down nothing harsh, nothing burdensome . . . But as we progress in this way of life and in faith, we shall run on the path of God's commandments, our hearts overflowing with the inexpressible delight of love.*

> —*RULE OF ST. BENEDICT*, PROLOGUE 45–46, 49

I know artists whose medium is life itself and who express the inexpressible without brush, pencil, chisel or guitar. They neither paint nor dance. Their medium is Being. Whatever their hand touches has increased life. . . . They are the artists of being alive.

—Frederick Franck

Materials needed: paper, markers in black, gold, and jewel-toned colors (like bright blue, red, or green).

This week, gather together all of the creations that have emerged during this course and sit with them for a while, allowing them to speak to you in a collective voice. Observe their invitations in the writing of your rule of life.

Consider revisiting one of the poetic forms we have used in past weeks—haiku, pantoum, blessing, psalm of praise, fairy tale, and openings such as "I am going to start living like . . ."—as a way of bringing some poetry to your rule. Each section might begin with a poem to encapsulate your commitment, or you might write your whole rule in poetic form.

Use the structure that feels most helpful to you. You might consider broad categories under which to make commitments to contemplative practice, creative expression, and the support of community.

Once your rule of life is complete, consider ways you might express it visually, creating a document that is sacred to you. Enter into this experience as an act of prayer. Using paper and a colored marker pen, draw borders along the edges of your pages. Draw flowered vines or spirals, stars and moons, or abstract and geometric shapes. Consider playing with a variety of different shapes and forms to begin highlighting the borders. Then write the words of your rule, perhaps a statement to highlight each commitment and then a few words to express how you will live this out. When you are done writing, take some gold or jewel-toned markers and fill in the loops of your letters to give them a feeling of illumination and honor.

Bless your rule and create a simple ritual for yourself as a way of marking your new commitments. Consider sharing it with a soul friend, spiritual director, or small community.

Eightfold Rule.
1. *Practice simplicity.*
2. *Pray unceasingly.*
3. *Create daily.*
4. *Treat my body as a temple.*
5. *Be still and just breathe.*
6. *Let your light so shine.*
7. *Live, love, laugh wholeheartedly.*
8. *Remember this.*

—REBECCA PISKURA

What Does It Take?
Intention to live fully aware of all of my senses
Hearing
Sounds of Nature around me
Cries of my gut
Music within my heart
Blessings of silence
Seeing
Beauty of each person
Oppression of sisters around the world
Allure of each natural season
Self within self
Touching
Dirt of the earth
Tools of creative expression
Books, old friends and new
Loved ones and strangers
Smelling
Fragrances of nature
Memories of joy and loss
Foods which nourish
Persons who have gifted me
Tasting
Foods from around the world
Hope unearthed in prayer

Homemade gifts from friends
Love received unbidden
Retreat happens
In moments of insight
During planned time away
With awareness of Grace
Any minute, hour, day or week.

—BARBARA LINDQUIST MILLER

THE ARTIST *and* MONK ARE ONE

The Monastic Spirit and the Pursuit of Everlasting Beauty

If, indeed, truth is beauty and beauty truth, then the monk and the artist are one.

Monasticism, in fact, cultivates the artistic spirit. Basic to monasticism are the very qualities art demands of the artist: silence, contemplation, discernment of spirits, community, and humility. Basic to art are the very qualities demanded of the monastic: single-mindedness, beauty, immersion, praise, and creativity. The merger of one with the other makes for great art; the meaning of one for the other makes for great soul.

It is in silence that the artist hears the call to raise to the heights of human consciousness those qualities no definitions ever capture. Ecstasies, pain, fluid truth, pass us by so quickly or surround us so constantly that the eyes fail to see and the heart ceases to respond.

*It is in the awful grip of ineffable form or radi-
ant color that we see into a world that is infinite-
ly beyond our natural grasp, yet only just beyond
our artist's soul. It is contemplation that leads an
artist to preserve for us forever, the essence of a
thing that takes us far beyond its accidents.*

—JOAN CHITTISTER

I hope that after reading these pages and engaging in the meditations
and explorations offered that you have begun to see how the artist and
monk are indeed one. Contemplative practice nurtures our ability to see
and hear the holy at work in the everyday. Creative expression gives form
to this vision and shares it with the world so that others can begin to discover God in their daily lives.

Thank you for taking this creative and contemplative journey with
me. I hope you are discovering how these practices spill over into everyday life so that you slowly become more aware of the presence of God
in each moment. The Jesuit theologian Karl Rahner described how each
moment can be potentially revelatory. This process helps to open up our
awareness so that we might receive the gift of revelation offered us with
each breath.

If you enjoyed this process, consider inviting a group of friends to
gather weekly or even monthly to engage in the creative exercises and
meditations together. A sample format for a session might be an opening
prayer, time for discussion on the reflections, and then some shared time
to pray lectio divina together or have one person lead the guided meditation. Close with a time to enter into the art, movement, and writing explorations and allow time for sharing from the experience.

The way of the monk is to bring full presence to each breath, gesture,
moment, action, or encounter. The path of the artist is to find beauty in the
world and to give it form and expression. When we weave them together
we create a life full of richness and possibility.

RESOURCES

Desert, Celtic, and Benedictine Spirituality

Casey, Michael. *A Guide to Living in the Truth: Saint Benedict's Teaching on Humility*. Ligouri, MO: Triumph Books, 2001.

Chittister, Joan. *Wisdom Distilled from the Daily: Living the Rule of St. Benedict Today*. San Francisco: HarperOne, 1991.

Chryssavgis, John. *Into the Heart of the Desert: The Spirituality of the Desert Fathers and Mothers*. Bloomington, IN: World Wisdom, 2008.

De Waal, Esther. *The Celtic Way of Prayer: The Recovery of the Religious Imagination*. New York: Image, 1999.

——. *Seeking God: The Way of St. Benedict*. Collegeville, MN: Liturgical Press, 2001.

Edwards, Tilden. *Living Simply Through the Day: Spiritual Survival in a Complex Age*. Mahwah, NJ: Paulist Press, 1998.

Fry, Timothy, ed. *The Rule of St. Benedict*. Collegeville, MN: Liturgical Press, 1982.

Jackson, Kenneth. *Studies in Early Celtic Nature Poetry*. Burnham-on-Sea, Somerset, England: Llanerch Press, 1995.

Lanzetta, Beverly. *Radical Wisdom: A Feminist Mystical Theology*. Minneapolis, MN: Fortress Press, 2005.

Merton, Thomas. *Love and Living*. New York: Harcourt, 1998.

———. *New Seeds of Contemplation*. New York: New Directions, 2007.

———. *Sign of Jonas*. New York: Harcourt, 1981.

———. *Thoughts in Solitude*. New York: Farrar, Straus and Girioux, 1999.

———. *Wisdom of the Desert*.

Moore, Thomas. *Meditations on the Monk Who Dwells in Daily Life*. New York: Harper Perennial, 1995.

Newell, J. Philip. *The Book of Creation: An Introduction to Celtic Spirituality*. Mahwah, NJ: Paulist Press, 1999.

Newman, Barbara, ed. *Voice of the Living Light: Hildegard of Bingen and her World*. Berkeley: University of California Press, 1998.

Norris, Kathleen. *The Cloister Walk*. New York: Riverhead Trade, 1997.

Schut, Michael, ed. *Simpler Living, Compassionate Life: A Christian Perspective*. New York: Morehouse Publishing, 2009.

Sellner, Edward C. *Finding the Monk Within: Great Monastic Values for Today*. Mahwah, NJ: Ambassador Books, 2008.

Steindl-Rast, David, and Sharon Lebell. *Music of Silence: A Sacred Journey Through the Hours of the Day*. Berkeley, CA: Ulysses Press, 2001.

Teasdale, Wayne. *A Monk in the World: Cultivating a Spiritual Life*. Novato, CA: New World Library, 2003.

Vest, Norvene. *Desiring Life: Benedict on Wisdom and the Good Life*. Boston: Cowley Publications, 2000.

———. *Friend of the Soul: A Benedictine Spirituality of Work*. Boston: Cowley Publications, 1997.

Waddell, Helen. *Beasts and Saints*. Grand Rapids, MI: W.B. Eerdmans, 1996.

Wiederkehr, Macrina. *Seven Sacred Pauses: Living Mindfully Through the Hours of the Day*. Notre Dame, IN: Ave Maria Press, 2008.

Wilkes, Paul. *Beyond the Walls: Monastic Wisdom for Everyday Life*. Chicago: ACTA Publications, 2010.

Creativity, Art, and Beauty

Beckman, Betsey, and Christine Valters Paintner. *Awakening the Creative Spirit: Bringing the Arts to Spiritual Direction*. New York: Morehouse, 2010.

DeLeon, Roy. *Praying with the Body: Bringing the Psalms to Life*. Brewster, MA: Paraclete Press, 2009.

Franck, Frederick. *Zen of Seeing: Seeing/Drawing as Meditation*. New York: Vintage, 1973.

Koren, Leonard. *Wabi-Sabi for Artists, Designers, Poets and Philosophers*. Point Reyes, CA: Imperfect Publishing, 2008.

Leonard, Linda Schierse. *The Call to Create: Listening to the Muse in Art and Everyday Life*. New Orleans: Spring Journal Books, 2009.

Loori, John Daido. *The Zen of Creativity: Cultivating Your Artistic Life*. New York: Ballantine Books, 2005.

May, Rollo. *The Courage to Create*. New York: W.W. Norton, 1994.

McGee, Margaret D. *Haiku—The Sacred Art: A Spiritual Practice in Three Lines*. Woodstock, VT: SkyLight Paths Publishing, 2009.

McGinnis, Ray. *Writing the Sacred: A Psalm-inspired Path to Writing and Appreciating Sacred Poetry*. Kelowna, British Columbia, Canada: Northstone Publishing, 2005.

Rilke, Rainer Maria. *Letters to a Young Poet*. Novato, CA: New World Library, 2000.

Sartwell, Crispin. *Six Names for Beauty*. New York: Routledge, 2006.

Wallas, Graham. *Art of Thought*. New York: Harcourt, Brace, 1926.

Additional Resources

Buechner, Frederick. *Whistling in the Dark: An ABC Theologized*. San Francisco: HarperOne, 1993.

Countryman, L. William. *Living on the Border of the Holy: Renewing the Priesthood of All*. Harrisburg, PA: Morehouse Publishing, 1999.

De Waal, Esther. *To Pause at the Threshold: Reflections on Living at the Border*. Harrisburg, PA: Morehouse Publishing, 2004.

John Paul II. *Letter to Artists*. Chicago: Liturgy Training Publications, 1999.

May, Gerald. "Entering the Emptiness." In *Simpler Living, Compassionate Life*, edited by Michael Schut. Harrisburg, PA: Morehouse Publishing, 2009.

Nouwen, Henri J.M. *Here and Now: Living in the Spirit*. New York: Crossroad Publishing, 2006.

Rumi, Jalal al-Din. *The Essential Rumi*. Translated by Coleman Barks and John Moyne. San Francisco: HarperOne, 1997.

Sarton, May. *Journal of a Solitude*. New York: W.W. Norton, 1992.

Taylor, Barbara Brown. *An Altar in the World: A Geography of Faith*. San Francisco: HarperOne, 2010.

Whyte, David. *Crossing the Unknown Sea: Work as a Pilgrimage of Identity*. New York: Riverhead, 2002.

Websites

Abbey of the Arts, http://www. AbbeyoftheArts.com
InterPlay, http://www.InterPlay.org
The River's Voice, http://www.RiversVoice.com

CREATIVE EXERCISES *and* MEDITATIONS

Week Four

Week Five

Week Six

Week Seven

Week Eight

Week Nine

Week Ten

Week Eleven

Week Twelve

LECTIO DIVINA PASSAGES

Christine Valters Paintner is the online abbess for Abbey of the Arts, a virtual monastery offering classes and resources on contemplative practice and creative expression. She holds a doctorate in Christian spirituality from the Graduate Theological Union in Berkeley and earned her professional status as a registered expressive arts consultant and educator from the International Expressive Arts Therapy Association. Paintner is the author of *Water, Wind, Earth, and Fire*, a columnist for *Patheos*, a retreat leader, and a supervisor for spiritual directors. She lives out her commitment as a Benedictine Oblate in the heart of Seattle with her husband and dog. Visit her online at www.abbeyofthearts.com.

Founded in 1865, Ave Maria Press,
a ministry of the Congregation of
Holy Cross, is a Catholic publishing
company that serves the spiritual and
formative needs of the Church and its
schools, institutions, and ministers;
Christian individuals and families; and
others seeking spiritual nourishment.

———⊷⊶———

For a complete listing of titles from

Ave Maria Press

Sorin Books

Forest of Peace

Christian Classics

visit www.avemariapress.com

ave maria press® / Notre Dame, IN 46556
A Ministry of the United States Province of Holy Cross